EMPOWERING
Your Ministry

Dr. Geoffrey V. Guns

TOWNSEND**PRESS**

Printed and bound in the United States of America

ISBN: 978-1-957621-69-2

Table of Contents

Introduction

Ministry, in this post-modern, technological era, has become increasingly more demanding and difficult. Christian ministry is more demanding because ministers face an array of new, complicated problems. Further, we are faced with dealing with a whole new type of individual and with needs that we have not had to deal with in the past. There are persons joining churches today who have never been connected to a church. They have never been baptized, nor do they understand the traditions of the Christian faith. They join as adults, becoming first-generation church members. In many instances, they are more affluent, better educated, and more demanding of quality ministry services and programs. They are likely to be loyal until someone else comes along with a better preaching style, bigger church, flashier television ministry, or something else new and novel that grabs their attention.

The new millennium church member is more likely to have a lower regard for spiritual authority and leadership. We are called to do ministry in an age when many of the people that we preach and teach have strong secular perspectives. It should come as no surprise that those we serve are not driven by an insatiable desire to serve the Lord at all costs.

In many instances, the people we seek to serve may have expectations that we may or may not be able to meet. Further, the demands of ministry are compounded by the desire and need of the preacher to be identified as having a successful ministry. Often, the demands for success in ministry run counter to our need to find fulfillment in the work that God has called us to undertake.

Indeed, as James E. Means has stated, the American pastor stands at a crossroads today.[1] Means stated that one of the two paths that we face leads to effectiveness in ministry, revitalization, and church growth. The other road leads to stagnation, increased secularization, and irrelevance on the part of the church.[2] Many of us are searching frantically for ministry models that we can use to spice up our ailing programs. We feel that if we don't "keep up with the Joneses," we will end up farther and farther behind our peers.

Ministers today must maintain a delicate balance between their desire for success and ministry effectiveness. If your deepest desire is to lead a ministry that is spiritually, biblically, and theologically effective, then you will face many difficulties in achieving that goal. What are some of the difficulties that we face as African American pastors today? First, there is a growing gap in real biblical literacy among the laity. African American Christians are simply not as theologically and biblically informed as we would like to think. The majority of our people neither read the Bible regularly nor consistently practice the spiritual disciplines. The evidence of the lack of biblical understanding is seen in the number of believers who do not attend Sunday school or weekly Bible study. There is a gap in the ability of many pastors to teach the Bible. Seminaries do not train the contemporary preacher how to teach the Bible today. Most seminaries teach many things related to the history and tradition of the Christian faith but very little in the way of empowering the inexperienced preacher to lead the congregation to real spiritual growth.

Second, we face stiff and growing competition from nondenominational movements. There is a gradual dilution of the collective strength of the African American Christian church because we are more likely to have an individual agenda than a cooperative community agenda. In some cases, younger pastors are opting not to affiliate with any denomination at all but, rather, start their ministry movements. This trend is pushing some Baptists to abandon their denominational labels in favor of neutral Christian markers. This is a growing trend among African American Baptists, which seems to be gaining momentum. I agree with Thom S. Rainer, whose insight on the decline of denominations is on target. He stated, "A second reason behind the decline of some denominations is that the institution and its bureaucracy gained priority over the local churches."[3] He said, "The denomination, begun initially as an entity for the churches, became a self-promoting body, forgetting that it was created to serve the local churches that carried its identity."[4] This is one of the big challenges facing the National Baptist Convention, USA, Inc. The denomination must develop an agenda and vision that considers the needs of struggling local churches or risk further erosions of strength.

Third, we face the challenge of dealing with shallow concepts of Christian spirituality. We must overcome the "made for TV" understanding of spirituality. A great deal of what people understand about the Christian faith comes from religious broadcasting. After all, our people spend more time listening to the radio than to us. There is nothing wrong with ministries that make use of the media. However, the danger is that in the attempts to draw viewers and raise revenue, they become more entertainment-focused and less biblical. Television dramatizes the faith, sometimes to the detriment of the local church.

Fourth, we face the challenge of a growing lack of discipline by the preacher. Many young pastors and preachers look at the older preachers and say, "I want that!" Yet, they fail to realize that success and effectiveness in ministry come with much sacrifice and discipline. It can take years to achieve true effectiveness in ministry. Young pastors and preachers must allow the Holy Spirit to grow the spiritual fruit of patience in their hearts. The harvest of an effective ministry will be the result of many years of planting and patiently waiting for the seeds to grow (see 1 Corinthians 3:6-8; Galatians 6:9).

Fifth, we face the ongoing challenge of growing congregations that may have little or no interest in deep religious study. A great deal of what you see on television is not serious biblical scholarship; it's the "gravy train." It's simple exposition without real examination.

There may be many other difficulties associated with achieving effectiveness in ministry. I am not implying that it is impossible to achieve ministry effectiveness. Instead, I am saying that ministry effectiveness is not as easily achieved today as you may think. However, I do believe that these are among the most exciting times in which to be doing ministry. We live at a point in history in which the world is changing daily. God has given us a message of hope and empowerment. We have an open door of opportunity to do a great work in the name of the Lord. That is what this book is about. It's about igniting your ministry and reaching the unlimited possibilities of God in your life.

Paradoxes in the Ministry

We face many paradoxes in ministry today. Conceivably, we may feel that length of service and tenure produce success in ministry. It would seem that the longer that one faithfully serves a congregation, the more likely he or she is to achieve greater ministry effectiveness. There are instances when pastors have remained with congregations for years and achieved very little ministry success. Why is this the case? There are many reasons for success or failure in ministry. They are not always easily defined and labeled. Many pastors struggle just to survive. Sometimes, a hostile church environment can be one of the contributing factors leading to the decline of the church's effectiveness in the community it seeks to serve. The pastor can become tired of the struggle and abandon any desire to achieve anything in a church. When you lose heart and become discouraged in ministry, it becomes easy to preside over maintaining the status quo. When the preacher is discouraged, the church suffers. On the other hand, we may be called to a church ready for change and new ideas, and everything just clicks for us. There have been instances when a preacher was called to a dying church and, within a few years, that church was one of the leading congregations in the city or town. What happened in his ministry that did not happen in the previous ministry? Here again, these things are not always easily defined.

I believe that we can be successful and effective in ministry, provided we do some of the right things. First, we must begin with clear expectations. If you start out believing that everything should and will go your way, you are headed for a great disappointment. Second, we must learn to allow the Holy Spirit to give us patience. Give the people time and yourself time to grow. Third, we must allow the Lord to give us a vision for the ministry to which He has called us. Fourth, planning and organization will be key elements in achieving any measure of ministry effectiveness. Fifth, teaching and preaching the Word of God will be the most important facets of your ministry. These are two skills we have to continuously work on and refine. We can never know enough about how to communicate effectively the Word of God, either through teaching or preaching. Lethargy, depression, despondency, and disappointment are not new to the servants of God. All whom God has called have had to contend with the demons of discouragement at some point in their ministries. Moses had to contend with continuous upheaval, rebellion, and doubters all the days of his tenure as Israel's leader (see Numbers 11:10-15; 14:2; 16:3; 17:5). The prophet Jeremiah became so despondent over the people's rejection and derision that he wanted to stop preaching God's Word.

> **O LORD, You have deceived me, and I was deceived;**
> **You have overcome me and I was deceived;**
> **I have become a laughingstock all day long;**
> **everyone mocks me.**
> **For each time I speak, I cry aloud;**
> **I proclaim violence and destruction,**
> **Because for me the word of the LORD has resulted**
> **In reproach and derision all day long.**
> **But I say, "I will not remember Him**
> **Or speak anymore in His name."**
> **Then in my heart it becomes like a burning fire**
> **Shut up in my bones;**
> **And I am weary of holding it in,**
> **And I cannot endure it.**
>
> **—Jeremiah 20:7-9** *(author's own paraphrase)*

God has always encouraged His servants to continue their work with the assurance that He would be with them (see Joshua 1:5-11; Jeremiah 1:5-11; Matthew 28:19-20). This is one of the key assurances of ministry; God promised to be with those whom He sends. When Moses voiced his inadequacies to the call of God, the Lord responded by reassuring him of His presence: **"And God said, 'I will be with you. And this shall be the sign to you that it is I who have sent you: When you have brought the people out of Egypt, you will worship God on this mountain'"** **(Exodus 3:12, NIV).**

The purpose of this book is to lay out a practical framework for beginning the task of developing an effective ministry. I am in no way making the presumption that by reading this single book, you will have all you need to develop an effective ministry. Instead, this is just a starting point for beginning the process. This is my contribution to an ever-increasing number of books on the subject of ministry in the coming millennium. I feel that my perspective is somewhat unique in that I write from the perspective of an African American Baptist preacher and pastor. My perspective has been shaped by my work as moderator of an association and as president of the Virginia Baptist State Convention. Further, I write from the perspective of a member of the board of directors of the National Baptist Convention, USA, Inc. A great deal of what is written about the African American Baptist church is written to point out what is wrong with it. There is a lot wrong with all churches. They are made up of humans who have fallen from grace. When we focus only on the problems that plague us in the ministry and the church, we continue the despair that many preachers feel. As a result of reading this book, I hope to set you on a road that will lead to greater ministry effectiveness in your ministerial context.

This is not a book about what is wrong with churches or preachers; rather, it seeks to provide clear direction on how God can best use our gifts in achieving His purpose in the world. During the more than twenty years that I have been engaged in full-time Christian ministry, I have had my share of heartaches, heartbreaks, and disappointments and committed my share of major and minor mistakes. Despite my failures, God is true to His word of being faithful and just to forgive and cleanse us from all unrighteousness (see John 1:29).

Chapter 1 will examine the concept of empowerment and its implications for creating a more effective ministry. In chapter 2, we will consider the call to ministry and what it means to acknowledge the claims of God upon our lives. In chapter 3, we will discuss ministerial spirituality as the framework for achieving ministry effectiveness. It is my prayer that after having read and studied this book, you will recognize the importance of having a clear vision for your ministry and the need for a biblically oriented mission statement. Throughout the book, I hope to provide some practical suggestions that you (the reader) may find helpful and applicable to your ministry context. God knows what will work where you are. Read my work and then seek the mind and will of God for your ministry. My mother always reminded me early in my ministry, "Son, you will have your greatest success where God sends you." Wherever we have been planted is where God chooses to work out His purposes for our ministry.

At the conclusion of your having spent precious time with me in reading this book, it is my most fervent prayer that the Lord will speak to your spirit and encourage you in your work of ministry. Ministry today is so radically different from what it was ten, twenty, or thirty years ago—yet we serve the same God of Abraham, Isaac, and Jacob. He is the same God of Moses, Aaron, and Joshua and the same God of our Lord Jesus Christ, who established the model for what our ministries should look like and be.

Chapter 1

What Is Empowerment?

"But you will receive power when the Holy Spirit has come upon you; and you shall be My witnesses both in Jerusalem and in all Judea, and Samaria, and as far as the remotest part of the earth."

—Acts 1:8 (NASB)

"Empowerment" is one of the new buzzwords of the twenty-first century. But precisely what is empowerment, and how does it relate to ministry? *Empowerment* can be defined as giving subordinates or followers the capacity to act on behalf of the organization. Empowerment is helping followers grow in their relationship with Jesus Christ to the extent that they are confident in their ability to serve the kingdom work effectively. Empowerment is helping others to grow and serve the ministry. Empowerment is helping followers discover their spiritual gift(s) and then encouraging the use of said gift(s) in the work of the ministry.

Donald Smith has written a very helpful book on the role of the pastor as a ministry empowerer.[1] The book is the result of a study that was conducted by the Office of Research of the Presbyterian Church (U.S.A.). The results of the study are relevant and may have some applicability to just about any ministry context. The study focused on identifying the factors that produce effective pastoral ministries. Smith noted that there is a distinct difference between an enabling ministry model and one that empowers.

Empowering is clearly different from, and much more than, "enabling." Several dictionaries include *enable* in the definition of *empower*. This seems to equate the two words. But the word *enable* has come to portray weakness rather than strength. In relation to alcoholics, it means to reinforce the alcoholic's weakness and thus the drinking problem. The cliche of an "enabling ministry" has led some pastors to move in the direction of a laissez-faire approach to their members. This leads only to weakness, not to power. Thus, for example, Lyle Schaller contrasts initiating leadership with enabling. His clear implication is that enablers do not initiate. Leadership contrasts with "enabling" (as it has come to be perceived). But it certainly is not antithetical to empowering. True leadership does not reinforce weakness and dependency. It empowers. *To empower individuals or institutions is to enhance their power* (italics added). It is to inspire, nurture, and serve them in such a way that they grow in their power to be and to do. In the context of the church, this means to communicate the Gospel in such a way that people receive the wholeness of redemption and the power of the Holy Spirit. That gives them the resources and the freedom to become all God intends them to be. That challenges them to move out into the world in witness and service. In the church as an organization, to empower is to release all the potential that God has placed within the church to become Christ's body in the world. This requires initiative from highly skilled and dedicated leadership.[2]

The goal of every congregational leader must be the empowerment of those whom he or she leads. Their empowerment ultimately means that the organization will be more effective. Our aim should be to harness and release the energy that lies dormant in the congregation.

Biblical Models of Empowerment

The Bible offers us an opportunity to study several leaders who empowered others to participate in ministry and congregational leadership. For our study, we will look at Moses. In Exodus 18:13-23, we have the classic biblical example of a "one-man show," as far as it relates to leading the people of God. Many modern African American congregations are led by "religious celebrities and superstars." These are men and women who see themselves as the stars of the church's ministry. They are unreachable and untouchable. They will not fellowship with other churches. They often refuse to have any denominational involvement or affiliation. If they were members of the denomination, when they reach a certain size, they cease to support. These are self-contained, religious loner kingdoms.

Moses was the sole leader of the children of Israel. He included none of the tribal leaders in the day-to-day work of leading the children of Israel. He simply did everything by himself. He provided all the spiritual guidance and counseling to the congregation. The task of leading such a large group was considerable. There were more than 600,000 men, besides the women and children, in the camp. Moses would sit and judge the people from sunrise to sunset all by himself (verse 13). His father-in-law, Jethro, priest of Midian, offered him some advice on how to save himself and the people (verses 17-18). Jethro encouraged Moses to concentrate on being the spiritual leader who brought the people's concerns before the Lord (verse 19). He was to **teach** them the statutes and laws of God and make known to them the way in which they were to walk, and the work they were to do (verse 20). Moses was advised to choose a core of leaders who could assist him in the work of leading the people. He was given specific traits to look for in the leaders. They were to be men who were able to do the work, feared God, were truthful men, and were not greedy for money (verse 21). These men were to be assigned specific groups of people to work with and lead; they were empowered to handle all the problems that came within the scope of their responsibility and authority—and whenever they encountered a major dispute, they were to bring the matter to Moses (verses 22-23). By taking this very practical approach to leadership, Moses would be able to live longer and endure the strains and stresses of congregational leadership.

Biblical Principles of Leadership Empowerment

There are several principles of congregational leadership empowerment that emerge from the passage about Moses. *Principles* are rules that are applicable in any situation, culture, or historical setting. Principles transcend time, place, and people. There are many timeless principles that we can learn from the ministry context of Moses that will aid and assist us in our various ministry settings. There may be other principles that you discovered in reading the passage about Moses. Take them and use them in your ministry context. The ones that I list are not the only principles that can be drawn from the passage; they merely represent my own reflection and thinking.

Principle Number One

The pastoral congregational leader is more effective when he can involve others within the congregation in the work of ministry.

Organizational effectiveness is increased as we share the task of leadership with others. Moses sought to do everything himself. His leadership style put him in the awkward position of assuming that he could do everything without the aid of others. Moses was on the road to burnout.

When we look at the ministry of Jesus, He clearly involved others in the mission on which the Father had sent Him. Jesus gathered around Himself a core group of men that He could train and inspire with a great and noble purpose (see Luke 5:1-11). He sent them out to serve as an extension of Himself and to exercise their gifts and spiritual authority (see Luke 10:1-20). When you are attempting to lead others in a great work, call around yourself followers who believe that God is the one sovereign, supreme ruler of the universe. It is imperative that those whom you seek to lead in ministry be committed to following the Lord first and you. In **2 Corinthians 8:5 (NASB)**, the apostle Paul made this statement about the Macedonian saints: **"and this, not as we had expected, but they first gave themselves to the Lord and to us by the will of God."** Pastors will need to recruit and equip supporters who will become totally committed to the Lord, your leadership, and your vision for the ministry. People want to be invited to join with you in achieving God's purposes. Don't be afraid to ask for help!

The primary task of the pastor/preacher is to equip and train workers for the work of the ministry. In the future, we will have a difficult time building effective ministries without the total commitment of others. Unless we are doing that we are not fulfilling our ministry. In **Ephesians 4:11-12 (NASB)**, the Holy Spirit gave specific gifts of leadership to the church for the task of equipping the saints. **"And He gave some as apostles, some as prophets, some as evangelists, some as pastors and teachers, for the equipping of the saints for the work of ministry, for the building up of the body of Christ."**

What is the function of the pastor/teacher? It is to prepare and outfit the saints for the work of service. Indeed, as Greg Ogden has stated, "An equipper's job is to build in people a belief that God has called them to ministry and to help them function in accordance with their identified call and giftedness."[3] The work of ministry involves more than just the pastor or other staff preachers. The Holy Spirit has given gifts of grace to each member of the body of Christ for the benefit of everyone (see 1 Corinthians 12:7). Your ministry is going to flourish to the extent that you can involve others in it.

Principle Number Two

Organizational effectiveness is increased when the congregational leader informs followers of their specific duties and responsibilities.

Diane Tracy has stated, "The very first and perhaps the most important thing you can do to give people power is to tell them what they are supposed to do. There can be no success unless you clearly explain to people what is expected of them."[4] When followers lack a clear understanding of what they are called to do and the work that they must undertake, they are likely to venture into areas outside of their responsibilities. Moses was advised by Jethro to show the newly appointed leaders their specific tasks (see Exodus 18:20).

Helping lay leaders to know their roles and jobs within the congregation will save you a great deal of heartache. Often, we assume that people know their jobs. They may have no idea of your expectations of them or what you think they should be doing.

Principle Number Three

Organizational effectiveness is enhanced when congregational leaders invest the appropriate authority in the hands of their followers.

Jesus was not afraid to share authority with His disciples. Jesus was also willing to submit to the authority of the Father (see Matthew 8:9). He did the things with which the Father was pleased. Jesus never sent His disciples out to do ministry without giving them the necessary spiritual resources, encouragement, and authority to be successful (see Matthew 10). As a result of what Jesus did with His disciples and for them, they were able to continue the mission of God upon His ascension and return to heaven (see Acts 1:11). "Leadership is lacking when it is not invested in followers in a way that empowers them to independently advance the cause."[5] You will increase your effectiveness when you invest appropriate authority to go along with assigned responsibility. Diane Tracy stated that "a manager empowers others by giving them authority equal to the responsibility assigned to them. People can fulfill the responsibilities of their jobs only to the extent that they have been given authority to do so."[6]

Authority is a major issue within the church. It is an especially volatile issue in many African American Baptist churches. The inability of young and older pastors to understand how it is acquired and how it is to be used is one of the key reasons for congregational conflicts. How do you acquire authority in ministry? First, by developing competence in ministry. It pays to know what you are doing. We often say to our people, "We need to study the Bible more." It's important that you be able to show them how to do it by first knowing yourself. Second, authority is acquired as we lead with a heart of compassion, pastoral concern, and care. I know that this is a continuous struggle for me. Many times, we can become so busy that we forget to provide some personal attention and care to our leaders and members. Third, if we do the right things, then time in office will enable us to acquire pastoral authority.

The preacher must be confident both in knowing the source of his/her authority and in the proper exercise of that authority. Moses' authority came from God's call to serve as Israel's liberating leader (see Exodus 3). According to Tracy, we severely limit people in the use of their abilities and talents when we do not give them the appropriate authority to carry out their assigned tasks.[7]

Principle Number Four

Organizational effectiveness is enhanced when the congregational leader provides sufficient training and personal development for followers.

Moses was advised to do two types of training. First, he was instructed to teach the leaders the Word of God, **"teach them the statutes and the laws" (Exodus 18:20, NKJV)**. Second, Moses was advised by Jethro to show them how to live and how to do the work that he was asking them to do (see verse 20). In the church, we must teach the Word of God and its mission mandate. Further, it is crucial that we help followers to develop the skills necessary to carry out their specific ministries.

Diane Tracy remarked, "Training is perhaps the most neglected of all the managerial functions and one of the most important. Many managers view training as a bothersome nuisance keeping them from their immediate goal, rather than a long-term solution to their problems."[8]

When we look at the record of the New Testament church, it is apparent that training and teaching were major responsibilities taken on by the apostles. They taught the disciples every aspect of life in the new covenant community (see Acts 2:41-47; 11:26). The apostle Paul made training and equipping of the church a key aspect of the ministry of spiritual leaders (see Ephesians 4:11-16). He reminded Timothy that it is the Word of God that is the foundation through which the man or woman of God is thoroughly equipped for every good work (see 2 Timothy 3:16-17).

Jesus is the supreme model of how training ensures the survival of our vision. He spent three years teaching His disciples and impregnating them with truths about God, the mission, and how they would be successful in their work beyond His stay on the earth. As we engage in the ministry of teaching, we can plant deep in the hearts and minds of those we lead the lessons that will last long beyond the class setting.

Application of the Principles

It is one thing for us to learn new principles of effective leadership; it is quite another to be able to put those principles into practice. To grow in pastoral and ministerial effectiveness, you will have to make a conscious decision to grow. Self-improvement is a personal matter. There is no one who can make us work. It's easy to grow fat and lazy in ministry. There is, in many instances, no one that we are required to report to or answer. The leader must develop and cultivate the discipline of work; without personal discipline, those whom you lead will soon detect your laziness and become like you or leave the church. Empowering our ministries is not a quick-fix remedy for slow-growing or no-growing churches. It takes time, and it begins with self-examination. You may want to take some time to work through some of these application principles with other colleagues in the ministry or alone. In this section, I want to lay out several practical steps to make these principles come alive or gain relevance in your own ministry context.

Application Principle Number One

Thoroughly review and seek to improve your own level of leadership competence. One of the most important developmental tasks of any preacher is to constantly place himself or herself under the microscope for personal self-examination. The apostle Paul encouraged the Corinthians to thoroughly look at themselves before seeking to examine others. **"Test yourselves to see if you are in the faith; examine yourselves! Or do you not recognize this about yourselves, that Jesus Christ is in you—unless indeed you fail the test?" (2 Corinthians 13:5, NASB).** We often assume that we have skills that we do not have. Effective organizational leadership is not acquired by just observing your pastoral mentor. There may be a great deal about his or her model that is flawed or that works in that particular ministry context that is not transferrable to any other setting. Regardless of how much you may like a particular song, not every song can be sung by every choir. They may not have the voices, musical talent, or leadership to sing it.

Ministry is contextual. That is, what is working across the street may not work on your side of the street. We have to look at our level of ability. God gives to each of us that which we can handle. It is according to our ability (see Matthew 25:15). Not all of us will be the pastor of a mega-church. Why? We simply may not have the ability to lead a very large congregation. The fact is that you may never lead a mega church. It will not indicate failure or that God has not blessed your ministry. God knows that not every church will be a large congregation. No one-size congregation serves every need.

There are some people that large congregations simply cannot reach or serve. The church in Smyrna was poor and small, yet Jesus commended them for their faithfulness (see Revelation 3:8-11). The church in Macedonia was a congregation that was under severe pressure and impoverished, and yet they were major contributors to the relief effort for the saints in Jerusalem who were living with a severe famine (see 2 Corinthians 8:1-6). Therefore, we must never put down the size of the work that God has given us nor seek to compare ourselves with other larger, expansive ministries.

Ask the following questions of yourself:

- How many books do I have in my library on congregational leadership, pastoral leadership, and/or organizational leadership?
- How many leadership courses or seminars have I personally attended?
- What are effective ministry models from which I can learn?
- How much leadership training does my congregation undergo annually?
- How many leaders do I mentor each year in the church?
- What leadership skills do I need to develop?
- What leadership skills do my followers need to develop?
- How can I best achieve the end of empowering the congregation I lead?
- What are my strongest leadership traits?
- What are my weakest leadership traits?
- Do I have a clear vision of the church's ministry?
- Is my concept of leadership biblically based?
- What is my understanding of servant leadership?
- How well do I delegate responsibility to others?
- Do I have a need to be in control of everything in my ministry?
- Am I prone to inviting others into full partnership with me?
- Given what I have just learned, do I consider myself to be a leader who empowers others?
- Are there persons to whom I can turn for godly counsel and wisdom?

Application Principle Number Two

Thoroughly review the leadership skills of your followers and congregational leaders. As we learned in the previous section about Moses, leaders can sometimes make assumptions about what their followers know. One of the most important tasks that you can engage in is evaluating the leadership competency of your followers. Many times, the reason why pastors encounter conflict within their congregations or among groups is that leaders do not have clearly defined lines of responsibility and authority. Once or twice a year, you need to evaluate the skill level of your leaders. Don't complain about what they do or do not do if you don't take the time to train them in what you want them to do. You will want to ask the following questions:

- How often are leadership courses conducted for the congregation's leaders?
- Who does the training of the leaders of the congregation?
- What types of training have been conducted for congregational leaders?
- What has been the observed result of the church's leadership training?
- What differences have you noticed between leaders who participate in training and those who do not?
- What value does your church place upon having trained leaders?
- How knowledgeable are your leaders about denominational matters?
- Are your leaders knowledgeable of the church's mission statement?
- Do the leaders of the congregation abuse or misuse authority?
- Do you find yourself at odds with your leaders over authority issues?
- Have the leaders of the congregation been trained to respect biblical authority and biblical leadership?
- Do your congregational leaders respect your office?
- Do your congregational leaders see you as the chief overseer set in the congregation by the Holy Spirit?

Chapter Summary

In this section, we developed a working definition of empowerment. *Empowerment* is helping others to discover their place in the ministry and giving them the tools and authority to exercise their spiritual gifts. We learned that when we empower others in the congregation, we lengthen and strengthen the reach of our individual ministries. Further, we looked at Moses, who served as our model of congregational ministry. We learned four principles of congregational empowerment from Moses. First, the pastoral congregational leader is effective only to the extent that he or she can involve others in the work of the ministry. Second, it is important for congregational leaders to inform followers of their specific job responsibilities. Third, congregational effectiveness is enhanced when leaders define the limits of authority that followers have in their hands. Fourth, congregational leaders improve the effectiveness of the church when followers are trained and developed for their ministries. We concluded this section by looking at two application principles. First, we must examine ourselves and our individual leadership skills. Second, we must examine the leadership skills of our followers. Only through self-examination can we begin the process of organizational change and improvement.

In the next chapter, we will look at the call to ministry and how our understanding of our call impacts our concept of ministry. Who we are and what we believe God has called us to do is crucial for developing an awareness of ourselves that is both spiritual and healthy.

Chapter 2

The Call to Ministry

"Who saved us and called us with a holy calling, not according to our works, but according to His own purpose and grace, which was granted to us in Christ Jesus from all eternity."
—2 Timothy 1:9 (NASB)

The absolute conviction with which God has called you to the work of the ministry is a key element undergirding the preacher's work.[1] The self-affirmation with which God has called us to perform a noble work empowers us for the trials and triumphs of ministry. Without a deep conviction of the call of God, our work can become burdensome and disheartening to the point that we will quit the ministry altogether. No man or woman should come to this work without a critical, honest, and thorough examination of the reality of the challenges of the work of the ministry. Many young men and women have announced a call to ministry without a careful critical evaluation of the seriousness of this work. The apostle Paul often spoke of his experiences in ministry. In 2 Corinthians 11, he defended his ministry against those who wanted to question his apostleship. In **verses 23-28**, he writes about the many hardships he endured for the cause of Jesus Christ *(paraphrased)*:

> **Are they servants of Christ? (I speak as if insane) I more so; in far more labors, in far more imprisonments, beaten times without number, often in danger of death. Five times I was beaten with rods, once I was stoned, three times I was shipwrecked, a night and a day I have spent in the deep. I have been on frequent journeys, in dangers from rivers, dangers from robbers, dangers from my countrymen, dangers from the Gentiles, dangers in**

the city, dangers in the wilderness, dangers on the sea, dangers among false brethren; I have been in labor and hardship, through many sleepless nights, in hunger and thirst, often without food, in cold and exposure. Apart from such external things, there is the daily pressure upon me of concern for all the churches.

Clearly, Paul's life was not an easy joy ride. He was often in constant danger of losing his life. He described some of his experiences in his letters. However, one of the biggest challenges was having to defend his call to be an apostle, which he wrote about on several occasions (see 1 Corinthians 9:1-23; Galatians 1:11-17).

I want to suggest several invalid reasons that some may have for believing that God has extended to them a call to ministry. First, we can be fascinated by the preaching and pulpit demeanor of our pastor-mentor and feel that God has called us to be just like him or her. Second, we can be impressed with the perceived trappings of influence, success, and power that some ministries produce. Third, we can be overpowered by congregational influences, wherein others will begin to announce for us our call to ministry. Granted, there is a place for congregational affirmation, but that comes after a lengthy process of personal spiritual growth. Fourth, we can feel the urge to continue in the family lineage of preachers, especially if our fathers or mothers are preachers. And there may be other influences throughout our lives, such as the urge to help others, the need to be loved, the need to make a difference in the world—all of these can be driving forces in our sense of call to ministry. But does that validate our call to ministry?

In this chapter, we will examine the call to Christian ministry. I want to limit our discussion to Christian ministry because the Bible has more to say about God's call to all men and women than space or time will allow us to faithfully consider. We will look at the Bible's teachings regarding the call to Christian ministry and what it means. Second, we will seek to understand in a fuller way how to discern the call of God for our lives. And lastly, we will consider the need to reexamine our call and whether or not God calls us from one ministry to another. This will not be a discussion of whether or not God calls women to ministry. Within the African American Baptist tradition, there are a variety of opinions and beliefs regarding women in ministry. We will not seek to settle that issue in this book. Our concern is to reach some understanding of what it means to be called by God to do the work of the ministry.

God's Call to Christian Ministry

The call to Christian ministry begins with an understanding of the mission of God which was manifested through the ministry of Jesus Christ. Christian ministry is an extension of the mission of Jesus Christ (see Matthew 28:18-20; Luke 19:10; Acts 1:8). When Jesus confronted Zacchaeus with the message of salvation and his need to repent, He stated what His mission was about: **"For the Son of Man has come to seek and to save that which was lost'" (Luke 19:10, NKJV).** On one occasion—when Jesus corrected and calmed an argument between His disciples over the question of seats in the kingdom—He told them what His purpose was: **"Just as the Son of Man did not come to be served, but to serve, and to give His life a ransom for many" (Matthew 20:28, NKJV).**

The ministry of Jesus consisted of preaching, teaching, and healing. Jesus preached that men and women should repent of their sins. **"From that time Jesus began to say, 'Repent, for the kingdom of heaven is at hand'" (Matthew 4:17, NKJV).** Jesus saw preaching as one of the most important aspects of His ministry. When people tried to limit the preaching ministry of Jesus to their communities, He reminded them that His work was universal in scope. **"But He said to them, 'I must preach the kingdom of God to the other cities also, because for this purpose I have been sent'" (Luke 4:43, NKJV).** Jesus spent a great deal of time not only preaching but also teaching His disciples and the multitudes of people who followed Him (see Matthew 5–7; Mark 2:13; 4:1).

Jesus taught with authority and not as the religious leaders of that day (see Matthew 7:29). Lastly, Jesus had compassion upon those who were sick; He healed them. Healing was a significant aspect of the ministry of Jesus (see Matthew 4:23-25; 8:1-3, 5-16). In healing hurting people, Jesus made them whole again (see John 5:1-15).

The ministry of Jesus was active. He did not limit Himself to one particular area in Palestine, but He traveled extensively throughout the region, reaching men and women with the Good News of God's grace. Wherever they lived, Jesus went to be with them and to minister to them. Jesus traveled to the northern regions of Palestine. He ministered to a single woman in Samaria (see John 4:1-26.). People were attracted to Jesus because He met their needs for healing and understanding of the Word of God.

> **Jesus was going about in all of Galilee, teaching in their synagogues and proclaiming the gospel of the kingdom, and healing every disease and every sickness among the people. And the news about Him spread throughout Syria; and they brought to Him all who were ill, those suffering with various diseases and severe pain, demon-possessed, people with epilepsy, and people who were paralyzed; and He healed them. Large crowds followed Him from Galilee and the Decapolis, and Jerusalem, and Judea, and from beyond the Jordan.**
> **—Matthew 4:23-25 (NASB)**

It was the work that Jesus actively engaged in that attracted large crowds of people to Himself (see Matthew 5:1; 8:1; 12:46; 14:22; 19:1-2). Jesus did not set out to become a popular, well-known preacher in Galilee. He simply sought to do the will of God the Father (see John 4:34; 6:38). As Jesus ministered to the brokenness of hurting people, they followed Him. Modern preachers face the constant threat of wanting to be popular. Popularity comes at the expense of being faithful to the work of the ministry. We must guard against wanting to appeal to and appease the people to whom we minister. We are called to live a well-pleasing life to God (see Colossians 1:9-10). Norman Shawchuck and Roger Heuser pointed out that the preacher sometimes faces conflicting desires: the desire to be poor in spirit and popular or magnificent.[2]

The Call to Follow Jesus

The call to Christian ministry is, first and foremost, the call to follow Jesus. No man or woman should even think of going into ministry without first acknowledging that we are called to follow Jesus Christ. Jesus never called men to follow noble ideas, great causes, or ambitious people. Rather, it was a clear call to follow Him (see Mark 8:34-38). From the ministry of Jesus and His call to His first disciples, we can discern some fundamental lessons about the nature of the call to Christian ministry.

- Jesus' call was to follow Him (Matthew 4:18-19).
- Jesus' call was to a specific work (Matthew 4:18-19).
- Jesus' call was to a new and different lifestyle (Matthew 5–7).
- Jesus' call was to a new work (Matthew 9:9).
- Jesus' call was to receive authority over unclean spirits, demonic powers, and spiritual wickedness and darkness (Matthew 10:1).
- Jesus' call was to face dangerous wolves (Matthew 10:16).
- Jesus' call was to new relationships (Matthew 12:46-50).
- Jesus' call was to costly discipleship (Matthew 16:24-26).
- Jesus' call was to servanthood (Matthew 20:26).
- Jesus' call was to make disciples of others worldwide (Matthew 28:19).
- Jesus' call was to feed the hungry (Luke 9:13).
- Jesus' call was to witness to the Resurrection (Luke 24:48).

- Jesus' call was to receive the anointing of the Holy Spirit (Luke 24:49).
- Jesus' call was to have faith in Him (John 14:11).
- Jesus' call was to abide in Him (John 15:5-10).
- Jesus' call was to love one another (John 15:12).

Jesus is the model of what our ministries should look like. It is from Him that we receive our direction. We are called to a life of absolute surrender to Him. If we are seeking to build a ministry that does not have Jesus as the starting point, we need to reexamine our motives.

Discerning the Call to Ministry

One of the questions I am asked occasionally is this: "How do you know if you have been called to preach?" I received my call to ministry at the age of twelve at Mount Pleasant Baptist Church in Norfolk, Virginia. It was on a Sunday afternoon after worship that I finally acknowledged that God had told me to go and preach the Gospel. Let me point out that the call did not come on a Sunday. The call came to me through an experience I had earlier in the year. Whether this was a vision, dream, or reality, I cannot say; what I remember is that one night, I was carried before the very throne of God, and it was there that I received the mandate to preach. The experience of the night on which this event took place in my life is vivid today, nearly thirty-eight years later. I remember it all quite well. The experience of my call to ministry is as fresh as Paul's was to him throughout his ministry; he referred to it on three separate occasions (see Acts 9:1-9; 22:1-21; 26:1-23).

How do you know when you have been called? This is a question that only the one who is called can answer. God calls all of us to the new life in Christ. He calls us to a life of hope and reconciliation. However, God also calls some from among us to be His consecrated servants who proclaim and teach His Word. Let's look at a few influences and people who can impact our call to ministry.

Family and Community Influences

Gardner C. Taylor remarked, "One's home and family can greatly influence one's call, positively or negatively."[3] Dr. Taylor does not believe that being the son of a pastor is the sole reason he entered the ministry. (I, too, am the son of a Baptist preacher.) Taylor stated further that those who grow up in a warm spiritual climate are more apt to see ministry as a possible lifestyle for themselves.[4] I believe the opposite can be said for those who grow up in a home where the parent serves in a hostile and stressful ministry situation: it can lead them away from the ministry and quite possibly away from the church.

John Polhill sees at least two biblical examples where persons may have been influenced by their family backgrounds to enter the service of the Lord. He cited the example of Samuel, who was dedicated to the service of the Lord by Hannah, his mother. He also notes John the Baptist, the son of Zechariah and Elizabeth—childless parents who gave John back to the Lord (see 1 Samuel 1–2; Luke 1:5-23, 67-80).[5]

We do not have to start with a family history of ministers as our ministry incubator. The prophet Amos stated that he did not have a prophet's upbringing when God called him. **"Then Amos replied to Amaziah, 'I am not a prophet, nor am I the son of a prophet; I am a herdsman and a grower of sycamore figs. But the LORD took me from following the flock, and the LORD said to me, "Go prophesy to My people Israel"'"** (Amos 7:14-15, NASB).

We can grow up in a church where the presence of the Lord is visibly demonstrated and accepted as a living reality and sense the call to ministry. I believe that a lot of what we believe about our responsibility to serve the kingdom of God stems from the environment of our congregational life. God does call us from periods of preparation in congregations where the Spirit is active, and God is honored and worshipped. Preparation for ministry does not all take place in seminary or Bible college. It takes many years for God to groom us for the one period in our ministries when we will have our greatest successes.

If we grow up in a church where the call to ministry and Christian service is highlighted and presented as responsible Christian service, we are more likely to see it as not just someone else's call but ours as well. In many African American Baptist churches, we have not always done a good job of highlighting the real need for young men and women to consider the work of foreign missions or institutional ministries (i.e. military, campus ministry, hospital chaplaincy, and penal institutions). Not all ministry takes place in the context of the local congregation.

Dramatic Life Experiences

Sometimes we can discern the call of God through major life experiences. God sometimes calls men and women to ministry using spectacular or dramatic events. There are several examples in the Old Testament of dramatic experiences where God appeared in some visible manifestation of Himself. They are more likely to be found in the Old Testament than in the New Testament. These experiences are appropriately called *theophanies*. In Exodus 3, Moses met God in the form of a bush that burned but was not consumed. He was then told to go and say to Pharaoh that God wanted His people released (Exodus 3:10ff). The apostle Paul had a dramatic experience of his call to ministry while on the road to Damascus (see Acts 9:1-9). He was overcome by a bright light and he heard a voice from the heavens telling him that he was working against God and he would fail. Paul spoke of it on another occasion during his ministry (see Acts 22:6-16). It was in the year of King Uzziah's death that Isaiah said that he saw the Lord (see Isaiah 6:1-8). Ezekiel had a very dramatic call. **"Now it came about in the thirtieth year, on the fifth day of the fourth month, while I was by the river Chebar among the exiles, the heavens were opened and I saw visions of God" (Ezekiel 1:1, NASB).** Sometimes, God cannot get our attention in any other way than through a dramatic experience.

The Gradual Call

Not everyone has had dramatic experiences during our call to ministry. Some of us do not know exactly when we were called. There may have been nothing dramatic or earth-shattering about our desire to enter the ministry. This is the experience of the persons who say that for some time, they have felt the urge to preach God's Word. We may discover that God has called us by developing our spiritual gift(s). One of the gifts of the Spirit is the gift of exhortation. We may have resisted the urges, hoping they would go away, but they did not. It finally reaches a point where you cannot resist any longer. We simply have to allow the Word of God to burst forth like the sun's rays after the storm clouds have hovered over us for days.

The Reluctant Call

John Polhill references a reluctancy to accept or acknowledge our call to ministry.[6] Jonah is perhaps the most well-known example of someone who was called by God to be a prophet, and he simply refused to carry the Word. Jonah was called to go and preach to a nation of people he hated. The Ninevites were people whom Jonah wanted to see sentenced to the extremes of God's wrath.

Some have seen in their call to ministry a deep sense of worthlessness (see Exodus 4:1-17; Isaiah 6:6-7).[7] The apostle Paul also felt a deep sense of his own unworthiness because he had been a persecutor of the church of Jesus Christ (see 1 Corinthians 15:9-11).[8]

Reevaluating Our Call to Ministry

Donald P. Smith stated that the deep conviction with which God has called us to ministry is one of the three major assurances undergirding Christian ministry. The second is an active spiritual life stimulated by the abiding presence of the Holy Spirit. The third is the loving support that we receive from others.[9] I am increasingly convinced that we all need to reexamine our call to ministry occasionally.

In the African American Christian experience, we usually equate the call to ministry with a call to pastor a congregation. Outside of the pastoral ministry, there are very few opportunities for young men and women to exercise their ministry gifts. The picture is starting to change. There are very few denominational jobs available in traditional African American Baptist denominations. In the state of Virginia, there are no African American Baptist district associations that employ a full-time staff director or anyone else for that matter. Many of the associations barely survive, given the limited amount of financial, pastoral, and programmatic support that they receive from convention churches. The same can be said for African American state conventions that may have hundreds of churches (listed on membership rolls) but receive very little real financial support. Conversations with many other state denominational leaders give me the same impression; they all paint the same grim picture of their state organizations' suffering from apathy and minimal support. In my work as a state convention president, I had very few resources available to conduct the work of our convention. The picture is no less the same when we look at the National Baptist Convention, USA, Inc. I do not want to generalize my experiences to all state conventions or Baptist associations, but I believe it is generally true. Thus, when the only career path we see is pastor, it is the only one we aspire to reach.

The National Baptist Convention, USA, Inc. must begin to create real denominational and ministry opportunities for young men and women. There is a great deal of talent that lies wasting away in local churches. We may have one of the largest pools of untapped human resources in the world. Our size does not belie our real potential. I want to suggest that you look at your ministry to see if there are other areas of service into which God would lead you. This, of course, represents a major challenge for district associations and state conventions.

Pastoral Longevity and Ministry Success

One of the major factors contributing to congregational effectiveness is pastoral longevity. African American pastors tend to remain with a local congregation for many years. It is not uncommon to hear of fifty-year pastoral tenures. However, is that always a sign of God's intention? Is God not free to call us or send us to other locations? Paul never stayed in any location longer than three years. There are positives and negatives that can be assessed for long and short pastoral tenures.

The longer you remain as the pastor of a church, the greater the probability that you will have an effective ministry. This gives the Lord time to allow the vision He has given us to be born and blossom. It took Moses forty years to prepare the children of Israel for Joshua to lead them across the Jordan River. When they left Egypt, they were not ready; they had been slaves for 430 years, and they did not know how to live as free men and women.

There is always the possibility that you could be a total failure as a pastor, even during a long tenure. The church could be a mismatch and be spiritually destructive for both the preacher and the people. Contrary to that, a short tenure does not give you the necessary time to implement meaningful, effective ministries. Donald Smith has suggested five things that pastors may want to do to reevaluate their call to a particular church.

- Initially discern with clarity God's call to pastoral ministry and a particular congregation.

- Constantly assess the needs of your people and the gifts needed with which to meet their needs.

- Annually clarify yours and the congregation's expectations of your ministry.

- Periodically revisit your calling with honesty and openness to change and adapt your approach to ministry to the work of the Holy Spirit.

- Regularly refine and cultivate the gifts necessary to meet the changing demands of ministry.[10]

Evaluating our ministry occasionally is vital to our continued development as preachers and pastors. Many seasoned pastors may resist the very suggestion that they engage in some sort of ministry assessment. It may not be pleasant, but it could be a key to personal growth in ministry. We live in one of the most exciting times in the Christian era. The skills that I received in seminary twenty years ago are not sufficient to sustain a vital and growing ministry today. I am convinced that many seminaries must undertake a major paradigm shift, away from what may be called traditional theological education to one that is more practice-oriented. By evaluating our ministry skills, we can discern our strengths and weaknesses and look for ways to improve our practices. What are some ways that we can improve our skills as pastors and ministers? Often, we fail to engage in lifelong learning.

- Participate in ministry seminars and training sessions that focus on ministry.
- Consider starting a ministry support group that spends time in prayer and study together with other preachers.
- Look for courses of study in local colleges or universities that might enhance your ministry skills.
- Seek out older or more experienced ministers who can mentor you and give you the spiritual guidance and support you need.
- Look for ways to encourage your spouse or help her to become involved in a support group for ministers' wives.
- Cultivate the discipline of personal study and development.

Elements of the Call to Ministry

In this section, we want to consider the elements of the call to ministry. These are single-sentence statements that capture some aspect of our call to ministry.

- God calls us to ministry despite our past failures, our handicaps, and our personal sense of unworthiness.

- God calls us to ministry based upon His standards and not those of society and the world.

- God calls us to ministry even though we actively engage in other pursuits.

- God calls us to ministry, where we face the possibility of confronting hostile people and situations.

- God calls us to ministry and equips us with the spiritual tools necessary to carry His Word effectively.

Application Principle Number One

Periodically, reassessing your call to ministry and reliving your experience of God's grace upon your life can be a great source of encouragement when the winds of trial come in your work.

We must never assume that God has given us an easy road to follow. Ministry drains us even when there are no major spiritual, personal, financial, or social problems within the congregation or your home. Sometimes, we must remind ourselves that God has called us for this work. Sometimes, when we are burdened in our spirit, we need to remind ourselves that we never called ourselves, but God called us to tend His flock. This enables us to become spiritually reliant upon God and not ourselves.

Application Principle Number Two

Seek to allow the Holy Spirit to lead you in areas where you can experience personal spiritual development and growth.

One of the biggest deceptions of Satan is to convince us who preach that we do not need to be spiritually fed and nurtured. Therefore, we rarely seek godly wisdom from senior or successful pastors until we have a problem. God has called us to be co-laborers together with Him. We are also co-laborers together with each other. Learn how to take care of yourself so that you can tend the flock over which God has placed you.

Chapter Summary

In this chapter, we have briefly examined the call to Christian ministry. We noted that our understanding of ministry must grow out of the model created by Jesus Christ. In this chapter, we came to understand that the call to Christian ministry is ultimately a call to follow Jesus. Further, we took a look at how to discern our call to ministry with some sense of clarity. Only we can authenticate our call with certainty. We noted that each of us needs to reevaluate our call to ministry periodically. It is especially vital for pastors to honestly evaluate their calls to serve particular congregations. Lastly, in this section, we took a look at five elements of the call to ministry. In the next section, we are going to see the importance of spirituality and its importance for the preacher's life.

Chapter 3

The Preacher and Spirituality

"Be on guard for yourselves and for all the flock, among which the Holy Spirit has made you overseers, to shepherd the church of God which He purchased with His own blood."
—**Acts 20:28 (NASB)**

What does a typical day of ministry look like for you? Does it start early with a review of the day's schedule and end late in frustration, with your wondering where the time went? After breakfast, do you rush to the church? Upon your arrival, you are met with ten new messages, three scheduled appointments, two counseling sessions, and two meetings later in the evening, not to mention the unscheduled drop-ins, telephone calls, and emergencies that crop up on a daily basis. This probably seems like an exaggeration; however, in reality, it is how a typical day can go for many pastors. Often, our days are crowded with "stuff." We are very busy doing ministry, exercising our gift, leading the congregation, and managing the enterprise we call the church. Being busy gives many of us a sense of self-importance. Preachers are among the busiest people I know and, well, we should be. We have so many human needs to meet, and members have problems that need our personal attention.

When the apostle Paul gathered with the elders of Ephesus on his final trip through Asia Minor, he encouraged them in their work of ministry (see Acts 20:17-36). He reminded them that the first responsibility that they had was to take care of themselves: *Be on guard for yourselves.* Unless the preacher takes care of himself, he cannot possibly hope to take care of the flock that God has placed under his care. How well do you take care of yourself? Are you so focused on your ministry that you have failed to see your own spiritual needs? In this section, we are going to look at the preacher and his spirituality. At the outset, we will develop a definition of *spirituality* and *spiritual formation*. We want to come to understand why developing a deeper spiritual life and relationship with the Lord Jesus Christ is crucial to the longevity and effectiveness of our ministry. Further, we will look at some of the signs of spiritual stagnation and how to recognize if we are going in the wrong direction.

Lastly, we will look at some of the things to which you and I need to give priority to be the preachers that God has called us to be.

What Is Spirituality?

What does it mean to be spiritual? In his letter to the Galatians, Paul wrote, **"Brothers and sisters, even if a person is caught in any wrongdoing, you who are *spiritual* are to restore such a person in a spirit of gentleness; each one looking to yourself, so that you are not tempted as well" (Galatians 6:1, NASB; italics added).** There are several implications regarding the statement about the church in Galatia. First, not everyone in the Galatian congregation was spiritual. Second, there are some situations that can come up in a congregation that require special people to deal with them. Third, spiritual people will deal with the fallen brother or sister in a manner that allows the person to be restored to the congregation and his or her proper place.

Norman Shawchuck and Roger Heuser noted that one of the greatest dangers facing the contemporary religious leader is "becoming so busy or so bored, so proud or so depressed, that the things they desire most, as well as their actions, go unexamined."[1] We are called to constantly seek a deeper and closer walk and relationship with Jesus Christ. It is the relationship with Christ that keeps us from falling into the traps of Satan—whose desire it is to "sift us as wheat" (see Luke 22:31). Therefore, we cannot begin to develop effective ministries without developing our interior lives. Shawchuck and Heuser remarked that churches want pastors who possess competent skills in ministry, but they also want pastors who possess inner character and integrity.[2] For many of us, it is easy not to schedule a real devotional time. We can become so busy with church work that we only read the Bible when it's time to prepare a lesson or sermon. Further, it is easy to be so overwhelmed by the demands of ministry that we become frustrated by and tired of the constant struggle of trying to keep up. Cultivating a deeply spiritual relationship with Jesus Christ enables us to overcome the spiritually draining aspects of ministry. Let's consider several definitions of *spirituality.*

> Spirituality is the means by which we develop an awareness of the Spirit of God in us and the processes by which we keep that awareness alive and vital, to the end that we become formed in the Spirit of Christ.[3]
>
> —Norman Shawchuck and Roger Heuser

> Spirituality is paying attention to the life of the spirit in us; it is going out to the desert or up to the mountain to pray; it is standing before the Lord with open heart and open mind; it is crying out, "Abba, Father"; it is contemplating the unspeakable beauty of our loving God.[4]
>
> —Henri J. M. Nouwen

> Spiritual development refers to the interaction of our efforts with those of the Holy Spirit in order to bring about strong and healthy Christian spiritual life in believers, congregations, and in the ministers who lead them.[5]
>
> —David S. Dockery & David P. Gushee

> **Therefore I urge you, brothers and sisters, by the mercies of God, to present your bodies as a living and holy sacrifice, acceptable to God, which is your spiritual service of worship. And do not be conformed to this world, but be transformed by the renewing of your mind, so that you may prove what the will of God is, that which is good and acceptable and perfect.**
>
> **—Paul (Romans 12:1-2, NASB)**

In each of the definitions of *spirituality* and *spiritual formation*, the emphasis is on cultivating the inner sanctuary of our hearts, minds, and spirits. The work that we are called to do is a spiritual work, and it cannot be effectively done unless the preacher is spiritually strong. We are engaged in a cosmic conflict and spiritual battle. Paul reminded the Ephesians of the nature of the struggle:

Finally, be strong in the Lord and in the strength of His might. Put on the full armor of God, so that you will be able to stand firm against the schemes of the devil. For our struggle is not against flesh and blood, but against the rulers, . . . the world forces of this darkness, against the spiritual forces of wickedness in the heavenly places.
—Ephesians 6:10-12 (NASB)

For though we walk in the flesh, we do not wage battle according to the flesh, for the weapons of our warfare are not of the flesh, but divinely powerful for the destruction of fortresses. We are destroying arguments and all arrogance raised against the knowledge of God, and we are taking every thought captive to the obedience of Christ, and we are ready to punish all disobedience, whenever your obedience is complete.
—2 Corinthians 10:3-6 (NASB)

There is nothing more vital to the long-term strength and vitality of your ministry than your personal spiritual growth. It is as impossible to think and believe that we can preach an effective, transforming Gospel without the Holy Spirit as to think a plane can fly without an engine. Dockery and Gushee remarked, "Your level of spiritual health and well-being will affect every aspect of your character and every aspect of the conduct of your ministry."[6] By simply refusing to pay attention to who we are inwardly and the state of our spiritual lives, we set ourselves on the road toward heartbreaking failure. Paul instructed Timothy to prepare himself for ministry by disciplining himself for godly living. **"Have nothing to do with worldly fables fit only for old women. On the other hand, discipline yourself for the purpose of godliness; for bodily discipline is only of little profit, but godliness is profitable for all things, since it holds promise for the present life and also for the life to come" (see 1 Timothy 4:7-8).**

Biblical Foundations of Spirituality

The New Testament, particularly the letters of the apostle Paul, helps us develop a clear understanding of what it means to live a spiritual life. In **Ephesians 5:18**, Paul wrote, **"And do not be drunk with wine, in which is dissipation, but be filled with the Spirit" (NKJV).** The apostle gave two commands in this verse. The first was "do not get drunk with wine." The reason why the Ephesians were not to get drunk with wine was because it leads to excess and wastefulness. Getting drunk is an artificial way to induce joy and pleasure. This form of exhilaration will not last. Rather, as a direct contrast to the first command, the apostle gave a second imperative command: "be filled with the Spirit."

The words of Paul were written in such a way that he encouraged the Ephesians to be filled continuously. The disciples were filled on the Day of Pentecost—but they were also filled on other occasions after that (see Acts 2:4; 4:8, 31). Every preacher needs the abiding presence and power of the Holy Spirit daily. Being filled with the power and presence of the Holy Spirit is a natural part of every believer's life, including the preacher's. We are filled for service and witnessing; it is never an end within itself. In fact, we cannot even claim to be spiritually healthy without the filling of the Holy Spirit. The prayer of every pastor/preacher should be that the Lord would fill him with the Holy Spirit daily. As we confess our sins and failures to God, we should continuously seek to be empowered repeatedly with the power that can only be supplied by the Holy Spirit.

In this part of our study, we are going to look at some of the Bible's teachings on spirituality. This will not be a complete study, but merely a review of what is a vital Christian doctrine. The doctrine of the Holy Spirit has either been overlooked by many Baptists or misunderstood. We are a community of faith created by the indwelling presence of the Holy Spirit. We have no life apart from the life that He gives to us.

What It Means to Be Spiritual

The word *spiritual* comes from a Greek word *pneumatikos* and it denotes that which has the quality and life of the Holy Spirit. In the New Testament, it denotes special endowments or gifts that are given to believers by the Holy Spirit (see Romans 12:6-8; 1 Corinthians 12–14; Ephesians 4:11-13). These gifts are given by the Holy Spirit to the church to be used to build up the body of believers for the work of ministry (see 1 Corinthians 12:7; Ephesians 4:12). Each believer is given a gift of grace to be used for Christian service and advancing the kingdom. "Spiritual" is used to describe a specific type of believer within the church (see 1 Corinthians 3:1; Galatians 6:1). It denotes a blessing from God that is not of this world (see Ephesians 1:3). Further, it denotes specific types of songs and music unique to the Christian experience and sung within the church (see Ephesians 5:19). There is spiritual wisdom and spiritual understanding that cannot be acquired through any other means than the Holy Spirit (see Colossians 1:9).

The Holy Spirit produces fruit which is an indication of an active and growing spiritual life (see Galatians 5:22-23). Healthy trees automatically produce healthy fruit. The growth of fruit is an indication that something is happening on the inside that is positive, powerful, and productive. When we are seeking to grow spiritually, Satan will try to use every tactic in his diabolical arsenal to stop it. He knows that if the preacher is anointed and filled with the power of the Holy Spirit, great things will happen in the church.

Jesus said that our fruits are an identifier of who we are and whose we are. He said that false prophets can be easily recognized by the fruit that they bear.

> **"Beware of false prophets, who come to you in sheep's clothing, but inwardly they are ravenous wolves. You will know them by their fruits. Do men gather grapes from thornbushes or figs from thistles? Even so, every good tree bears good fruit, but a bad tree bears bad fruit. A good tree cannot bear bad fruit, nor can a bad tree bear good fruit."**
>
> **—Matthew 7:15-18 (NKJV)**

The new life in Jesus Christ is a reflection of the presence of the Holy Spirit's power and presence in our lives. The Holy Spirit is the divine agent of the new birth (see John 3:5-7). Each of us receives the Holy Spirit at the moment of conversion. At that very moment, we are baptized into the body of Christ (see Acts 2:38; 1 Corinthians 12:7, 13). The word *baptism* comes from the Greek word *baptisma,* which means to be immersed into something.[7] It is through baptism into the death of Jesus Christ that we take on the new life into the death of Jesus Christ (see Romans 6:4; 2 Corinthians 5:17; Ephesians 4:22-24). Baptism is a symbolic act that indicates a deeper spiritual change inwardly. It is the new life that we have in Jesus Christ that frees us from the domination and dominion of sin and death (see Romans 6:6-7). As a result of our new life, we are to present our bodies as instruments of righteousness and not as tools of Satan. Sin no longer has any dominion in the life of the believer (see Romans 6:12-13). The power of God makes us strong!

The believer has been set free from the power of the law of sin and death. God delivered us from condemnation when Jesus Christ died on Calvary's Cross for the sins of the world (see Romans 8:1). His death brought us into a new state of peace with God and access to the Father (see Romans 5:1-2). Because we are free from the law of sin and death, we are summoned to a new way of living—life in the Spirit. **"For the law of the Spirit of life in Christ Jesus hath made [us] free from the law of sin and death" (Romans 8:2, KJV)**. The word *law* in the verse just cited refers to the principles that govern our lives. Paul was referring to living in the domain and under the dominion of Satan. When we live under Satan's authority, we are subject to his rule and laws. It is the work of the Holy Spirit to set us free to live authentically as children of God. The Holy Spirit releases us from Satan's dominion and kingdom.

When we are born again and filled with the Spirit, we receive a new mental orientation. The Holy Spirit transforms our minds and renews our thinking (see Romans 12:1-2). Our minds are now set on the things of the Spirit, which produces life and peace (see Romans 8:6). We lose all obligations to the flesh and the sin it produces (see Romans 8:12). The flesh is our lower nature that always wants to control us by keeping us in bondage to Satan. We are led by the Spirit in all things. We walk in the Spirit. We operate in the Spirit (see Romans 8:12-14). We conduct our ministries under the inspiration and control of the Holy Spirit. When we order our lives according to the Spirit's control, we will make fewer personal errors in judgment that can all but cripple and destroy our ministries.

The Spirituality of Jesus

It is clear from the Gospels that Jesus nurtured His Spirit. The ministry of Jesus consumed a great deal of His time and energy. Jesus was constantly involved in preaching, teaching, and healing many types of diseases and sicknesses. He faced the constant pressure of the crowds and the looming reality of the Cross. Yet, He found time to work and maintain a meaningful relationship with His Father in heaven (see Mark 1:35; Luke 6:12). If Jesus had to pray and seek the will and mind of the Father, how much more do you and I need to do the same? If He had to have time alone before making key decisions, how much more do we need to have time alone? If He spent the night in prayer, how much more do we need to spend more time in prayer?

Shawchuck and Heuser identify what they see as the three key elements of the spirituality of Jesus.[8] First, they state that Jesus carried out His ministry in the context of a small, intimate covenant community. Second, Jesus established an order of priorities for His public and private life. Third, Jesus practiced six "graces" in His life: prayer, fasting, the Lord's Supper, the Scriptures, spiritual conversation, and worship in the Temple.[9]

When we look at the spiritual practices of Jesus, it is obvious that one of the keys to His spiritual energy was His commitment to the will of the Father and His willingness to submit Himself to God's will (see Luke 22:42). Jesus provides for us a model of how to stay spiritually healthy amid the busyness of ministry. I want to look at some of the key spiritual practices of Jesus. We are going to look at two aspects of His spiritual discipline: prayer and fasting.

Jesus and Fasting

In Matthew 4:1-11, one of the first challenges of His infant ministry was temptation by the devil. Immediately after His baptism (by John the Baptist), Jesus was led into the wilderness by the Holy Spirit to be alone. During the forty days He spent in the wilderness, He practiced the discipline of fasting. **"Then Jesus was led up by the Spirit into the wilderness to be tempted by the devil. And after He had *fasted for* forty days and forty nights, He then became hungry" (Matthew 4:1-2, NASB).**

One of the questions that you may have is this: "How necessary is it for me to practice fasting today?" Jesus mentioned how fasting was to be carried on by His disciples (see Matthew 6:16-18). He did not provide specific instructions on how to fast. He assumed that His disciples did and would continue to practice fasting.

You may ask, "What spiritual benefits are there for me in practicing fasting?" Fasting is a spiritual discipline. Without discipline in our lives, we run the risk of getting out of spiritual condition. Fasting is not only practiced by Christians but also by various religions and people who want to either lose weight or develop a deeper spiritual discipline in their lives. "Fasting is a most tangible and practical way of surrendering to God and allowing the Holy Spirit more control in our lives."[10] Tan and Gregg point to several purposes of fasting:[11]

- Fasting strengthens prayer.
- Fasting enables us to better hear the voice of God.
- Fasting aids us in self-denial and self-discipline.
- Fasting helps us face persecution.
- Fasting is a way of humbling ourselves before God.
- Fasting strengthens us against temptation.
- Fasting helps us minister to the needs of others.
- Fasting helps us express love and worship to God.

I first learned about fasting from my mother and father who practiced it religiously. My mother practiced it more so than my father, who is a Baptist pastor. My mother sees fasting as a form of self-mortification and sacrifice. It helps the believer develop a deeper dependence upon the Lord.

The Prayer Life of Jesus

Prayer was one of the dominant and most prevalent recorded spiritual practices of Jesus in the Gospels. You and I cannot have powerful ministries without the practice of relational prayer. By that I mean having a prayer life that nurtures our relationship with God the Father. In the Gospels, we see patterns in the life and ministry of Jesus that show us that His ministry was not just about miracles; rather, it was about doing what God the Father had sent Him to do. The Gospels give us a clear description of the practice of Jesus' prayer life.

And after he had sent the multitudes away, he went up into the mountain apart to pray: and when even was come, he was there alone.

—Matthew 14:23 (ASV)

But Jesus Himself would often slip away to the wilderness and pray.

—Luke 5:16 (NASB)

Now it was at this time that He went off to the mountain to pray, and He spent the whole night in prayer with God.

—Luke 6:12 (NASB)

Now it happened that as he was praying alone, the disciples were with him. And he asked them, "Who do the crowds say that I am?"

—Luke 9:18 (ESV)

And it came to pass about eight days after these sayings, that he took with him Peter and John and James, and went up into the mountain to pray.

—Luke 9:28 (ASV)

[But Jesus was saying, "Father, forgive them; for they do not know what they are doing."] And they cast lots, dividing His garments among themselves.

—Luke 23:34 (NASB)

It's very obvious from these passages that Jesus had an active prayer life. Jesus would often spend long hours in prayer. He prayed all night prior to choosing the twelve men who would be His disciples (see Luke 6:12-13). On some occasions, He invited His disciples to go along with Him to the mountain to pray. Jesus had a specific location where He would go and spend time in prayer alone. Jesus would spend long hours in prayer prior to making any major decisions.

Jesus not only prayed, but He also taught His disciples how to pray (see Matthew 6:5-15). We should teach our leaders not only the importance of prayer, but also, *how* to pray. We must teach them the elements of prayer, the purpose of prayer, and the power of prayer, and provide them books of prayers for study. Jesus prioritized prayer in His ministry. On one occasion, His disciples asked Him to teach them how to pray (see Luke 11:1). He taught them to pray for their enemies and those who hated them (see Matthew 5:44). He prayed for them and their future success (see John 17). Prayer was not just something that Jesus did because it was expected that a religious man would pray. Rather, it was the life blood that kept His ministry alive, powerful, relevant, and connected to the will of the Father. Prayer empowers the preacher for committed and courageous service to the kingdom of God.

If you want your ministry to come alive with new vitality, begin to spend serious time in prayer. Prayer places us at the complete disposal of God. Prayer opens our minds and hearts so that we might hear from Him and to talk to Him. God seeks to use us for greater Christian service and works (see John 14:11-14).

Prayer is our key to finding clarity in His will for our lives. Let me make some practical suggestions that may help strengthen your prayer life:

- Develop a personal prayer life.
- Create opportunities for your leaders to pray together.
- Conduct periodic prayer vigils in the church.
- Consider a prayer retreat as part of your leadership training.
- Conduct prayer seminars and encourage prayer groups in the church.
- Read and conduct a personal study of prayers in the Bible and the occasions that gave rise to them.
- Spend some time studying the prayer lives of great men and women of prayer by reading their books.

The Signs of Spiritual Stagnation

Most of us who are engaged in full-time and part-time ministry neglect the disciplines that keep us spiritually alive and strong to our own detriment. We all agree that there are activities that we should engage in and there are some that we can just as well do without. Often, we may find ourselves doing the things that we can do without and leaving off the things that are essential to our ministries. We can create situations wherein our priorities become misplaced and misaligned. When we begin to neglect the spiritual dimension of our lives and become consumed with the work of ministry and what we do, we are headed for spiritual stagnation and, quite possibly, spiritual death. How do you recognize spiritual stagnation?[12]

I want to suggest that spiritual stagnation does not take us by surprise. Rather, it is a condition that develops over time. Spiritual stagnation is an imperceptible process. It is like drifting in the ocean. You cannot discern movement because of the vastness of the sea. Satan can strip and sift us without our ever realizing what is going on. We may not recognize the signs of its development in us. Signs give us insight into our current location or condition. They are like road markers that tell us where we are on the highway.

Pastors are not the only ones subject to spiritual stagnation. Church leaders, workers, and associate pastors and ministers can experience spiritual stagnation as well. Pastoral assistants and associates can be beaten up by hostile members and insecure senior pastors who are jealous and afraid that their talents and abilities are stifled.

When I am asked by associate ministers how they can overcome the feelings of despair in their budding ministries, there are several suggestions I give them. First, *reaffirm and confirm your loyalty to your pastor-mentor*. Let him know that you support his ministry by making yourself available for service. Second, *practice loyalty*. Many times, young ministers are enticed by members who are hostile toward the pastor to work against him. Third, *be willing to do the small things in ministry.* Too many times we want to do the big things and grab the headlines for ourselves. Fourth, *be patient and give the Lord time to round out your rough edges and develop your ministry.* Fifth, *don't be so eager to preach; learn what the ministry is about first.*

Anyone in the service of the Lord is subject to experience spiritual stagnation. Let me share a few of the signs with you:

- The work of ministry becomes boring and unappealing.
- The work at the church is one constant fight.
- You have lost your joy for the things of God and the ministry.
- You have isolated yourself from your family and other preachers.
- You feel alone and abandoned in the church.
- You do not have a sense of personal satisfaction with your ministry.
- You are contemplating looking for another profession or job.
- Preaching and teaching the Word has become laborious and taxing.
- There is a loss of joy in worship and in leading worship.
- You are overcome by feelings of deep depression and rejection.
- You find yourself thinking more and more about infidelity.
- Your desire to fight the good fight is all but gone.
- There is no time for private devotion and Bible study.
- Prayer is something you preach about but do not practice.
- The work of ministry overwhelms you to the point of despair.
- You wish that God had never called you to preach.
- You develop a spirit of cynicism toward the ministry.
- Ministry is more a joke than a living reality in your life.
- Your family life is nonexistent or marginal, at best.
- You begin to lose all sexual desires for your spouse.

Four Causes of Spiritual Stagnation

I want to make some observations regarding what I consider to be four of the major causes of pastoral spiritual stagnation. Some of these observations are from my personal experience and others are drawn from research and literature in the field.[13] In some ways, they are related to the signs or symptoms of spiritual stagnation.

No preacher is immune from spiritual stagnation. Two of the greatest giants in the Bible struggled with their work for the Lord. On at least one occasion, both wanted to die so as to be relieved of the burden of their calling (see Numbers 11:10-17; 1 Kings 19:1-4). Moses was so overwhelmed by the trials and burdens of leading the children of Israel that he wanted God to take his life. Moses felt that God had been unfair with him by giving him so much responsibility and no help (see Numbers 11:1-15). Elijah heard that Jezebel was out to take his life and fled into the wilderness (see 1 Kings 19:1-4). The trials of ministry can overwhelm and envelope us in a continuously rising tide of internal struggle and pain. What are the four major causes of spiritual stagnation?

Loss of Personal Spiritual Intimacy with God

What happens to the congregation when the preacher has no devotional life? What happens to the spiritual growth of the people when the preacher has no personal time *with* or *for* God or the things of God? It becomes apparent over time, and the congregation will suffer. You can lose contact with God amid the hustle and bustle of doing ministry. This became crystal clear to me during the time when our church was undertaking a major construction project. I became absorbed in raising money, meetings with building committees, architects, contractors, bankers, trustees, and all the other cumbersome chores that are associated with church construction projects.

I try to share with pastors who are involved in construction projects that building anything is time- and energy-consuming. They can take years to become reality. Church construction projects can wear down your spirit and bring about serious confrontations among the congregation over their viability.

Many African American pastors stop attending local associations, state and national conventions, and other helpful conferences all for the sake of saving money for the construction project. We delay salary increases, believing that the few dollars we save the church will make them more appreciative and generous when the project is complete. You may have good intentions but, believe me, it's a bad decision. I went three years without a salary increase and, in the process, my purchasing power declined by more than 15 percent. I did not hurt the church—I hurt my family's quality of life. When we engage in these kinds of hapless actions it leads to future frustration in our ministries. In effect, what you are doing is laying the groundwork for spiritual stagnation.

There were two areas of my life that suffered severely during the thirteen years that we were involved in our construction project: my devotional and private time with the Lord, and my family life. I needed both to help me keep things in perspective. I came close to losing both. As with Samson—who did not know that the Spirit of the Lord had left him—the Holy Spirit was not actively guiding my ministry. Samson made the mistake of losing intimacy with God and was tricked by Delilah into thinking that he was immune from spiritual and moral failure. **"She said, 'The Philistines are upon you, Samson!' And he awoke from his sleep and said, 'I will go out as at other times and shake myself free.' But he did not know that the LORD had departed from him" (Judges 16:20, NASB).**

We can get too busy for the things that really matter the most in our personal lives and spiritual development. It is important to do the things that keep our ministries spiritually strong and vibrant. One of the challenges that Jesus issued to the church of Sardis was to "remember" what they were and had been (see Revelation 3:3). Spiritual intimacy is your contact point with God. Lose that and you have lost the source of your spiritual authority and power. In their book *Spiritual Wholeness for Clergy,* Donald R. Hands and Wayne L. Fehr pointed out the following:

> Parallel to this alienation from self very often is a lack of real *personal* relationship to God. The alienation from God is concealed by the cleric's immersion in 'the work of God'—teaching, preaching, visiting the sick, praying with others, presiding at liturgy. While sincere, this kind of activity can coexist with an almost complete absence of private, personal presence to God.

> Ordained ministers can live for years on the level of the 'objective,' church-mediated faith (what 'we' believe), without reflecting much on their personal history with God, without any heartfelt personal love involvement with God.

> This kind of 'existential distance' from God, as already indicated, is usually linked with an alienation from one's own deep personal center. People like this live 'on the surface,' much of the time simply maintaining a false self that is pleasing and impressive to others.[14]

Intimacy with God is what allows us to have the compassion and concern necessary to touch the hearts of those to whom we seek to minister.[15] Jesus often spent time alone, reflecting, praying, and meditating over the great work of human redemption (see Matthew 26:39). Jesus knew that His personal time alone with the Father was the key to His public demonstrations of strength. Jesus is a model of how to develop intimacy with the Father. We should see it as the glue that holds our ministry together. We must seek to cultivate our personal, private time alone with God.

Remedies for the Loss of Spiritual Intimacy

- Reassess and reevaluate your spiritual life.
- Begin to set aside daily time for private devotion, prayer, and Bible reading.
- Seek God's forgiveness for neglect of your spiritual development.
- Share with leaders in the church your need for spiritual growth.
- Learn to be less hands-on and controlling; delegate more.
- Develop the habit of reading devotional classics.
- Set aside private time with your spouse for prayer and Bible reading.
- Seek or start a spiritual growth group.
- Read and study and teach about the spiritual disciplines.
- Study the Gospels with the intention of learning from Jesus how to cultivate a deeper spiritual relationship with the Father.
- Put into practice what the Spirit teaches you.
- Cultivate a childlike openness to the ministry of the Holy Spirit.
- Seek God's guidance for every minor and major task.
- Teach your leaders how to make decisions based on reaching a spiritual consensus.
- Attend conferences and seminars that help you grow in ministry.

Putting the Church Ahead of Your Family

For some, this may appear to be heresy. But how can you make such claims when Jesus clearly taught that the work of His disciples had to take priority over everything and everyone, including one's family (see Luke 9:57-62)? Indeed, Jesus did make radical demands upon His disciples about absolute loyalty and devotion to Him and His cause (see Mark 8:34-38). He still makes radical demands upon those of us who have cast their lot and lives with Him. The apostle Paul willingly gave up all claims to personal success and achievement for the one great goal of knowing Jesus Christ (see Philippians 3:4-14). We are still summoned to sacrifice all for "the prize of the high calling."

Too often, everything, everyone, every cause, every problem, and every new set of circumstances take precedence over the preacher's personal family life. Sometimes, preachers will spend holidays attending the family gatherings of members to the neglect of his or her own family. We will miss major family events to look to meet the needs of members, all under the banner of doing our job as pastor of the church. Paul reminded Timothy that overseers have to ensure that their own families and marriages are well-managed, and that care is taken to safeguard their relationships with their spouses and children (see 1 Timothy 3:2-4).

A host of problems can develop when the preacher has an unhealthy marriage. First, the preacher who does not respect his marriage is living in disobedience to the Word of God. The Word of God holds up marriage as the most sacred of human relationships (see Genesis 2:18-25; Matthew 19:3-8; Ephesians 5:20-33; Hebrews 13:4; 1 Peter 3:7). Second, he can find himself unintentionally involved in an unholy relationship outside of his marriage. This is the extreme case and is worthy of mentioning. The more the preacher absents himself or herself from the home, the greater becomes the risk of falling into the trap of Satan. We must remember constantly the Bible's teachings regarding the primacy of marriage and the awfulness of adultery and fornication (see Genesis 2:18-25; Ephesians 5:21-33; Proverbs 6:27-35). Paul reminded Timothy to flee the onslaught of lust and temptation (see 2 Timothy 2:22). The preacher must constantly recognize that Satan wants to use our own lusts to entice us to sinful conduct (see James 1:14; 4:1).

Third, by neglecting our family life, we run the risk of not being a father or mother to our children. There is no more heartbreaking statement that a preacher's child can make than to say that their father or mother is always absent or gone. We are especially vulnerable to the trap of teaching others how to rear their children while neglecting to rear our own. There are many of us who have been very successful in the ministry, but miserable failures at home. Many pastors (whose children have reached maturity) often say that their biggest regret is not spending more time with their sons and daughters. Preachers are encouraged and exhorted to be models of good conduct in every way (see Titus 2:7).

Fourth, family neglect can lead to the most serious of problems: the loss of our personal integrity. Many preachers have respect in the one place it matters most—at home. The preacher's name and reputation are his or her most important asset. An ancient Hebrew sage remarked, **"A good name is to be more desired than great wealth; favor is better than silver and gold" (Proverbs 22:1, NASB)**. Lose your name and reputation and you lose the power of your preaching and personal testimony. America has become a nation in which integrity is in short supply. Lovett H. Weems Jr. remarked thusly:

> Religious leaders have paralleled other discredited public leaders. Too often we have seen the same patterns—advocacy of social policies for others with which they themselves are unwilling to live, greed and love of money, failures of personal morality, and one-issue zealotry. The examples are numerous and painful. This era is hardly the first time that this has been the case for religious leaders, but it is a reality of our time of which we must take account.[16]

Remedies for Putting the Church Ahead of the Family

- Reconnect to your spouse (if you have lost contact).
- Plan special times for you and your spouse to spend alone.
- Set a regular day to have lunch with your spouse.
- Resolve not to conduct church business when you are at home.
- Help the congregation understand the importance of your family.
- Take time to romance your spouse.

- Reconnect to your children (if you have lost contact).

- Establish a time for family prayer and Bible reading.

- Always take a family vacation.

- Send e-mail cards and letters to family members.

- Guard your family time zealously.

- Try to avoid having to work at home in the evenings.

The Constant Trauma of Congregational Conflict

Conflict is an inevitable part of the pastoral ministry. Anyone who seeks to lead the people of God must be prepared to face and resolve conflicts. Even among Jesus' disciples arose internal squabbling over seats of prominence within the coming kingdom of God (see Mark 10:35-45). The first Christian churches faced a variety of conflicts over issues that we would hardly give any credence to today. In the Jerusalem church there arose a dispute between the Jewish and Hellenistic widows over the daily distribution of food (see Acts 6:1-4). When Gentiles began to accept Jesus Christ as Lord and Savior, there arose a question over circumcision, the use of meat that had been sacrificed to idols, and the place of the Law (see Acts 15:1-29).

There were individual conflicts among Christians, such as the one between Paul and Barnabas over the status of John Mark. Barnabas was desirous of taking John Mark along on the next mission trip. Paul did not think that he should go along with them (see Acts 15:37-38). **"And there arose a sharp disagreement, so that they separated from each other. Barnabas took Mark with him and sailed away to Cyprus" (Acts 15:39, ESV).**

Church conflicts erupt over a variety of situations and issues. Therefore, never be surprised when they spring to life. Some can be major and require a great deal of prayer and help to overcome them. Others can appear to be minor and erupt into catastrophic nightmares for the preacher and his family. Often, conflict erupts over the failure of the people of God to understand their place in the divine economy of God's kingdom. Many congregations are out of order spiritually and are prime targets for Satan's influence and presence.

Many conflicts can be resolved with fervent prayer and a committed spirit of conciliation and compromise. Yet, we must remember that no conflict is resolved without some pain and difficulty. A great many conflicts could be avoided if church leaders better understood how conflict begins and possessed conflict-management skills. Many pastors have been the source of their own problems. Sometimes, just the way that we handle problems and situations can produce a climate of conflict. We can be stubborn and closed to hearing the people just as Rehoboam was to take wise counsel from the men who stood with his father, King Solomon (see 1 Kings 12:1-20). James E. Means offers some helpful advice to pastors for dealing with conflict.

> Avoid no-win situations. Pastors who learn the skills of interpersonal relationships do not allow themselves to be caught in no-win situations. Novices frequently find themselves in a position where they feel forced to choose sides with part of a congregation against another part, thereby offending and alienating many. Fence-sitting sometimes is ridiculous and not always possible, but on the other hand, too many pastors engender conflict by taking sides unnecessarily and allowing themselves to be pressed into a no-win stance, a position sure to offend a sizable portion of the congregation.[17]

What happens when you are in constant conflict with congregational leaders or small, highly organized special interest groups, who have made the destruction of your ministry their agenda? There are pastors who have dealt with long-term, deep-seated opposition. When the Jews returned from Babylonian exile and began the work of rebuilding the Temple, a group of locals sought to frustrate their efforts and work. **"Then the people of the land discouraged the people of Judah, and frightened them from building, and bribed advisers against them to frustrate their advice all the days of Cyrus king of Persia, even until the reign of Darius king of Persia" (Ezra 4:4-5, NASB).** The opposition in this case was not discouraged nor were they worn down by time. They continuously and ruthlessly stifled the rebuilding of the Temple for nearly sixteen years. They engaged in a variety of tactics designed to discourage the Jews. They wrote letters to the king of Persia accusing the Jews of being a rebellious people (Ezra 4:6ff.). The work on the Temple was halted!

When I was an army officer, one of the most important lessons I learned about battlefield survival had to do with visibility. If the enemy can see you, he can kill you. If you can see the enemy, you can destroy him. Pastors must learn real survival skills for effective ministry to take place in their churches. C. Lloyd Rediger has written an excellent book entitled *Clergy Killers: Guidance for Pastors and Congregations Under Attack,* in which he makes several key points about clergy survival.

> Because clergy killers typically target clergy (or perhaps another authority figure in church), they had better learn survival skills. This seems incongruous, for pastors tend to think that because their role and intentions are so noble, no one will attack them. But pastors must come to terms with diversity and critics, and learn how to negotiate differences. Pastors must learn survival skills, for they may encounter clergy killers. And if they do, noble intentions, Christian love, and negotiation will not save them. Even if pastors are willing to sacrifice themselves, they share responsibility for defending congregations, because clergy killers are perfectly willing to destroy congregations in their efforts to destroy pastors.[18]

Rediger offers some very helpful suggestions for dealing with clergy-killer conflicting situations.[19]

- Believe that it is possible for some to want to destroy you.

- Understand that your denomination typically has little power or inclination to save you from clergy killers.

- Learn the danger signals and patterns of behavior of clergy killers.

- Be aware that prevention is far better than reaction in dealing with clergy killers.

- Learn that building relationships in the congregation is key to preventing clergy killer attacks and provides a protective synergy.

- Accept the fact that evil and mental disorders are present in the church.

- Expect the attacks of clergy killers to have serious negative effects on your congregation and loved ones. Therefore, your survival skills are also important for their protection and should be taught to all of them as well.

- Learn that awareness and survival skills need not produce paranoia, nor rob you of the joy of ministry. They simply aid you to function in ways appropriate to contemporary reality.

You must remember that leaving a congregation is not always in the will of God for you and that ministry. Sometimes we must remain in a church to help the church learn how to deal with offensive and demonically controlled and demonically driven individuals. You must recognize that in many of these conflict situations, you are up against a deeply entrenched spiritual force that is out to destroy the witness of the church and the preacher.

Many African American pastors tend to break away from a troublesome church situation and start a new ministry. Rather than work through difficult issues, we will leave altogether with a few dozen or a few hundred people and begin anew. In some cases, this may be appropriate. The new church may thrive and grow. More than likely, it will be years of struggle. Some of the people who left to form the new ministry may return to the former church. Make sure that the Lord is leading you to start a new ministry out of an old ministry before attempting to do so.

I believe that we must learn group development skills that will help us manage conflict creatively. Jesus never ran from a conflict situation; He simply used it to further the Gospel. George O. McCalep Jr. remarked that one of the most important things for churches to do is to prioritize building healthy relationships within the church.[20] Most conflicts start because of personality clashes between the preacher and the people. Generally, it is over what God wants to do or what the preacher perceives as the direction for the church. We must learn how to remove ourselves from the center of the conflict. Jesus was a master at this.

The Failure to Practice Godly Living

What is godliness? Should the members of the church expect us to live and lead godly lives? Are the imperative commands of the New Testament "to be holy" applicable to the preacher's life? How does godly living help shape our ministry? The apostle Paul reminded Timothy that it was important for him to practice godliness among the believers he led. He wanted his son in the ministry to be a "good minister" of the Lord Jesus Christ.

> **In pointing out these things to the brothers and sisters, you will be a good servant of Christ Jesus, constantly nourished on the words of the faith and of the good doctrine which you have been following. But stay away from worthless stories that are typical of old women. Rather, discipline yourself for the purpose of godliness; for bodily training is just slightly beneficial, but**

**godliness is beneficial for all things, since it holds prom-
ise for the present life and also for the life to come.
—1 Timothy 4:6-8 (NASB)**

Paul pointed out the absolute importance of the preacher's being
sound doctrinally and spiritually. The spiritual growth and life of the
local congregation depends on the preacher's spiritual strength. If the
preacher is weak, the church will be weak. If the preacher is spiritually
impotent, the church will be spiritually impotent. If the preacher lacks
spiritual discernment and courage, the church will lack spiritual discernment and courage. The congregation mirrors its leadership.

Paul made several statements about what makes for a good minister
of Jesus Christ:

- He is willing to confront false teaching.
- He is constantly nourished on the words of the faith.
- He follows sound doctrine, avoiding wives' tales and fables.
- He practices the discipline necessary for godly living.

"Godliness" comes from the Greek word *eusebeia* and literally
means "to be devout, denotes that piety which, characterized by a
Godward attitude, does that which is well-pleasing to Him."[21] Paul
used the Greek word *entrepho* (nourished), which means to be reared
or brought up in something.[22] We must train ourselves for spiritual
development and godliness. Piety and the devout life must be the
norm in the life of the preacher. Does this mean that the preacher has
to live a sheltered and monastic life? No! I am not saying that. What I
am saying is that we need to begin to address the issues that relate to
the loss of spiritual confidence that people have in the ministry today.
We must walk our talk daily. It's not enough to stand and preach on
Sundays and teach on Wednesdays and forget who we are called to be
at other times.

We can have such great success in our ministry that we can begin to think that we are the cause of the people's coming to worship. We can begin to feel that we are the reason why the Holy Spirit is manifesting Himself in such powerful ways in the lives of the people we lead. We can begin to think that the church owes its life to us. Paul reminds us that we must not think more of ourselves than we should. **"For through the grace given to me I say to everyone among you not to think more highly of himself than he ought to think; but to think so as to have sound judgment, as God has allotted to each a measure of faith"** (Romans 12:3, NASB).

The church can be running over with people who are excited about the programs and the excitement generated by the worship, and nothing truly transformative and redemptive is happening in their lives. They are spiritually dead, and they may not even realize it. The preacher can be dead spiritually and still have all the trappings of a successful ministry in place.

We are only the earthen containers of the power of God. God's power is independent of us! Paul reminded the Corinthians of this very fact: **"But we have this treasure in earthen vessels, that the excellency of the power may be of God, and not of us"** (2 Corinthians 4:7, KJV). Preaching and teaching have transformative power only when we live out our creeds and doctrine. We are called to be practitioners of the Gospel we preach and teach to others (see Ephesians 4:1; James 1:22-23). Whatever we do, we must remember whose servants we are! **"For you were bought at a price: therefore glorify God in your body"** (1 Corinthians 6:20, NKJV).

Signs of a Godless Life

No fall from grace is sudden. It is a gradual process that unfolds and envelops us over time. The apostle James remarked, **"But each one is tempted when he is carried away and enticed by his own lust. The when lust has conceived, it gives birth to sin; and sin, when it has**

run its course, brings forth death" (James 1:14-15, NASB). What are the signs that we are living a godless life? A godless life is one without God's presence and power. It is a life that is characterized by hopelessness and despair (see Ephesians 2:11-12).

One significant example of a man of God who took the wrong road is Samson. In him can be seen the life of a man who violated the Word of God by revealing the source of his strength to Delilah (see Judges 16:13-19). You are leading a godless life or headed for one when the following actions are present in one form or another in your life:

- When you seek to fill your heart and mind continuously with unwholesome desires and lusts.
- When you are not troubled by your sins and moral failures.
- When you can openly flaunt your sinful and immoral behavior publicly without any shame or guilt.
- When you no longer have a desire nor inclination to preach about sin and the absolute need for repentance and forgiveness.
- When you are driven by your own desires for status and success and not the demands of committed discipleship commanded by our Lord Jesus Christ.
- When you no longer have a fear of the wrath and judgment of God upon your life and actions.
- When you are willfully and intentionally manifesting the lust of the flesh described in Galatians 5:19-20.
- When you no longer have a desire for personal repentance or contrition for your moral failures.

You can probably identify many more signs of a godless life or a life that is absent of the presence and power of God. There is nothing more pathetic than for a preacher to be empty and void of God's dynamic, transformative, and redemptive presence in his/her life.

Remedies for a Godless life

- Recognize that your life is out of control and under the law of sin.

- Repent and seek the forgiveness of God.

- Seek counsel and help from a godly friend or senior minister.

- Seek and ask for the forgiveness of your family and church.

- Get spiritual and professional counseling for your problems.

- Find a colleague to whom you can be accountable.

- Resist the first signs of temptation.

- Maintain a good reputation in the community you serve.

- Don't be naive about the impact of flirting.

- Seek help from your spouse about handling members of the opposite sex.

- Never counsel with women (men) alone in the church or at their private homes.

- Recognize where your personal weaknesses are and seek spiritual help.

Chapter Summary

In this chapter, we examined the preacher and his (her) spirituality. We are often faced with many demands that pull us away from the essentials of spiritual development. Spirituality is cultivated when we do the things necessary to keep our relationship with God alive and vital. The chapter also included a discussion on the spiritual life of Jesus and how He was able to stay focused and strong in His exhausting work of ministry. Jesus engaged in several of the spiritual disciplines. He was especially given to all-night prayer.

We examined the signs of spiritual stagnation. *Spiritual stagnation* is the noticeable absence or lack of measurable spiritual growth in our lives. It results when we move away from the practice of the disciplines of the faith—the things that keep us strong and vibrant. There are four major causes of spiritual stagnation. First, the loss of personal spiritual intimacy with God. Second, putting the church ahead of your family. Third, the constant trauma of church conflict. Fourth, the failure to practice godliness. These causes of spiritual stagnation are interconnected and there will not be one without the others (in whatever form that takes).

It is absolutely necessary that we spiritually take care of ourselves. God has called us to a great work, and it need not become the source of continuous frustration. While it is not without its frustration, still it has great rewards because the fruit we bear will last beyond our lifetimes. It will reproduce itself in eternity.

For Further Reading

Biersdorf, John E. *How Prayer Shapes Ministry.* Bethesda, MD: Alban Institute, 1992.

Briner, Bob, and Ray Pritchard. *The Leadership Lessons of Jesus: A Timeless Model for Today's Leaders.* Nashville: Broadman & Holman Publishers, 1997.

Brink, Kurt. *Overcoming Pastoral Pitfalls.* St. Louis: Concordia Publishing House, 1997.

Brown, Daniel A., with Brian Larson. *The Other Side of Pastoral Ministry: Using Process Leadership to Transform Your Church.* Grand Rapids, MI: Zondervan Publishing Co., 1996.

Ezell, Rick. *Ministry on the Cutting Edge: Maintaining Pastoral Effectiveness and Personal Authenticity.* Grand Rapids, MI: Kregel Resources, 1995.

Flynn, Leslie B. *How to Survive in the Ministry.* Grand Rapids, MI: Kregel Publications, 1992.

Grenz, Stanley J., and Roy D. Bell. *Betrayal of Trust: Sexual Misconduct in the Pastorate.* Downers Grove, IL: InterVarsity Press, 1995.

Guns, Geoffrey V. *Church Financial Management: A Practical Guide for Today's Church Leaders.* Franklin, TN: Providence House Publishers, 1997.

———. *Spiritual Leadership: A Guide to Developing Spiritual Leaders in the Church.* Lithonia, GA: Orman Press, Inc., 2000.

Gushee, David P., and Walter C. Jackson. *Preparing for Ministry: An Evangelical Approach.* Grand Rapids: Baker Books, 1998.

Hands, Donald R., and Wayne L. Fehr. *Spiritual Wholeness for Clergy: A New Psychology of Intimacy with God, Self and Others.* Bethesda, MD: Alban Books, 1994.

Harris, Forrest E., Sr. *Ministry for Social Crisis: Theology and Praxis in the Black Church Tradition*. Macon, GA: Mercer University Press, 1993.

Harris, James H. *Pastoral Theology: A Black-Church Perspective*. Minneapolis, MN: Augsburg Fortress Press, 1991.

Henderson, Perry E., Jr. *The Black Church Credit Union*. Lima, OH: Fairway Press, 1990.

Herman, Robert D., and Associates. *The Jossey-Bass Handbook of Nonprofit Leadership and Management*. San Francisco: Jossey-Bass Publishers, 1994.

Johnson, Ben Campbell. *Pastoral Spirituality: A Focus for Ministry*. Philadelphia: Westminster John Knox Press, 1988.

Johnson, Joseph A., Jr. *Proclamation Theology*. Shreveport, LA: Fourth Episcopal District Press, 1977.

Kouzes, James M., and Barry Z. Posner. *Credibility: How Leaders Gain and Lose It, Why People Demand It*. Foreword by Tom Peters. San Francisco: Jossey-Bass Publishers, 1993.

Lane, Eddie B. *The African American Christian Man: Reclaiming the Village*. Dallas, TX: Black Family Press, 1998.

Lincoln, C. Eric, and Lawrence H. Mamiya. *The Black Church in the African American Experience*. Durham, NC: Duke University Press, 1990.

Long, Eddie. *Taking Over: Seizing Your City for God in the New Millennium*. Lake Mary, FL: Charisma House, 1999.

Malphurs, Aubrey. Foreword by Haddon W. Robinson. *Developing a Vision for Ministry in the 21st Century*. Grand Rapids, MI: Baker Books, 1992.

Marshall, Tom. *Understanding Leadership*. Grand Rapids, MI: Baker Books, 1991.

McCalep, George O., Jr. *Faithful over a Few Things: Seven Critical Church Growth Principles.* Lithonia, GA: Orman Press, 1996.

Means, James E. *Effective Pastors for a New Century: Helping Leaders Strategize for Success.* Foreword by Bill Hull. Grand Rapids, MI: Baker Books, 1993.

Murdock, Mike. *The Leadership Secrets of Jesus.* Tulsa, OK: Honor Books, 1997.

Nouwen, Henri J. M. *Reaching Out: The Three Movements of the Spiritual Life.* New York: Phoenix Press, 1975.

Proctor, Samuel D., and Gardner C. Taylor, with Gary V. Simpson. *We Have This Ministry: The Heart of the Pastor's Vocation.* Valley Forge, PA: Judson Press, 1996.

Rediger, G. Lloyd. *Clergy Killers: Guidance for Pastors and Congregations under Attack.* Louisville, KY: Westminster John Knox Press, 1997.

Reed, Gregory J. *Economic Empowerment Through the Church: A Blueprint for Progressive Community Development.* Foreword by C. Eric Lincoln. Grand Rapids: Zondervan Publishing House, 1994.

Shawchuck, Norman, and Roger Heuser. *Leading the Congregation: Caring for Yourself While Serving the People.* Nashville, TN: Abingdon Press, 1993.

Smith, Bucklin & Associates. *The Complete Guide to Nonprofit Management.* New York: John Wiley & Sons, Inc., 1994.

Smith, Donald P. *Empowering Ministry: Ways to Grow in Effectiveness.* Louisville, KY: Westminster John Knox Press, 1996.

Smith, J. Alfred Jr. *Falling in Love with God: Reflections on Prayer.* Bible Study Applications by Colleen Birchett. Chicago, IL: Urban Ministries, Inc., 1997.

Tan, Siang-Yang, and Douglas H. Gregg. *Disciplines of the Holy Spirit: How to Connect to the Spirit's Power and Presence.* Grand Rapids, MI: Zondervan Publishing House, 1997.

Tracy, Diane. *10 Steps to Empowerment: A Common-sense Guide to Managing People.* New York: Quill William Morrow Company, 1992.

Weems, Lovett H., Jr. *Church Leadership: Vision, Team, Culture, and Integrity.* Nashville, TN: Abingdon Press, 1993.

Wolf, Thomas. *Managing a Nonprofit Organization.* Illustrated by Barbara Carter. New York: Fireside Books, 1984.

Endnotes

Introduction

1. James E. Means, foreword by Bill Hull, *Effective Pastors for a New Century: Helping Leaders Strategize for Success* (Grand Rapids, MI: Baker Book House, 1993), 13.

2. Ibid.

3. Thom S. Rainer, *Giant Awakenings: Making the Most of 9 Surprising Trends that Can Benefit Your Church* (Nashville, TN: Broadman & Holman Publishers, 1995), 11.

4. Ibid.

Chapter 1: What Is Empowerment?

1. Donald P. Smith, *Empowering Ministry: Ways to Grow in Effectiveness* (Louisville, KY: Westminster John Knox Press, 1996), ix-x.

2. Ibid., 11.

3. Greg Ogden, *The New Reformation: Returning the Ministry to the People of God* (Grand Rapids, MI: Zondervan Publishing Co., 1990), 98.

4. Diane Tracy, *10 Steps to Empowerment: A Common-sense Guide to Managing People* (New York: Quill William Morrow Company, 1992), 16.

5. Bob Briner and Ray Pritchard, *The Leadership Lessons of Jesus: A Timeless Model for Today's Leaders* (Nashville, TN: Broadman & Holman Publishers, 1997), 77.

6. Tracy, 31.

7. Ibid., 32.

8. Ibid., 65.

Chapter 2: The Call to Ministry

1. Donald P. Smith, *Empowering Ministry: Ways to Grow in Effectiveness* (Louisville, KY: Westminster John Knox Press, 1996), 157.

2. Norman Shawchuck and Roger Heuser, *Leading the Congregation: Caring for Yourself While Serving the People* (Nashville, TN: Abingdon Press, 1993), 33.

3. Samuel D. Proctor and Gardner C. Taylor, with Gary V. Simpson, *We Have This Ministry: The Heart of the Pastor's Vocation* (Valley Forge, PA: Judson Press, 1996), 2.

4. Ibid.

5. John Polhill, "Toward a Biblical View of Call," in *Preparing for Christian Ministry: An Evangelical Approach*, by David P. Gushee and Walter C. Jackson (Grand Rapids: Baker Books, 1998), 73.

6. Ibid., 74.

7. Ibid.

8. Ibid.

9. *Empowering Ministry*, 157.

10. Ibid., 168.

Chapter 3: The Preacher and Spirituality

1. Norman Shawchuck and Roger Heuser, *Leading the Congregation: Caring for Yourself While Serving the People* (Nashville, TN: Abingdon Press, 1993), 36.

2. Ibid., 37.

3. Ibid., 39.

4. Quoted in Shawchuck and Heuser's reference cited, 39.

5. David S. Dockery and David P. Gushee, "Spirituality and Spiritual Growth," in *Preparing for Christian Ministry: An Evangelical*

Approach, by David P. Gushee and Walter C. Jackson (Grand Rapids: Baker Books, 1998), 84.

6. Ibid., 81.

7. Floyd H. Barackman, *Practical Christian Theology: Examining the Great Doctrines of the Faith*, Third Edition (Grand Rapids: Kregel Publications, Inc., 1998), 205. There is a great deal of confusion or difference of opinion regarding the baptism of the Holy Spirit among believers. There is one school of thought which is reflected in the Pentecostal doctrine that the baptism of the Holy Spirit is a "second blessing" or work of grace that each believer is to seek. This is based upon the reading of Acts 19:1-7. The controversy is further fueled by the belief that the evidence of the Holy Spirit's presence is speaking in an unknown tongue. There is no scriptural, apostolic, or post-apostolic evidence to suggest that this was a New Testament church practice. Believers were never commanded by Jesus or His followers to seek the Holy Spirit, but to receive Him as the gift of the Father. The baptism of the Holy Spirit as a subsequent act of grace is a doctrinal tenet of the Full Gospel Baptist Church movement. It is a largely "Bapticostal" religious movement which seeks to espouse a charismatic flavor among Baptist churches. I believe that all Christians are Pentecostal and charismatic. We are all the product of what God did on the Day of Pentecost and we have all received the gifts of God's grace.

8. Shawchuck and Heuser, *Leading the Congregation*, 46-48.

9. Ibid.

10. Siang-Yang Tan and Douglas H. Gregg, *Disciplines of the Holy Spirit: How to Connect to the Spirit's Power and Presence* (Grand Rapids, MI: Zondervan Publishing House, 1997), 127. This is an excellent book and I strongly recommend it as a basic introduction to the spiritual disciplines.

11. Ibid., 130-134. There are several biblical references to fasting and I certainly commend them to you for your spiritual development and understanding.

12. The symptoms of spiritual stagnation that are presented reflect some the feelings that I encountered during a very difficult period in my ministry. After reading the work of Ben Campbell Johnson, I developed a separate list. See Ben Campbell Johnson, *Pastoral Spirituality: A Focus for Ministry* (Philadelphia: The Westminster Press, 1988), 17-18.

13. See Ben Campbell Johnson, *Pastoral Spirituality: A Focus for Ministry* (Philadelphia, PA: Westminster John Knox Press, 1988); Daniel A. Brown with Brian Larson, *The Other Side of Pastoral Ministry: Using Process Leadership to Transform Your Church*, foreword by Jack Hayford (Grand Rapids, MI: Zondervan Publishing Co., 1996); Donald R. Hands and Wayne L. Fehr, *Spiritual Wholeness for Clergy: A New Psychology of Intimacy with God, Self and Others*, foreword by Susan Howatch (Bethesda, MD: The Alban Institute, Inc., 1993); Kurt Brink, *Overcoming Pastoral Pitfalls* (St. Louis: Concordia Publishing House, 1997); George O. McCalep Jr., *Faithful over a Few Things: Seven Critical Church Growth Principles*, foreword by J. Alfred Smith Sr. (Lithonia, GA: Orman Press, 1996; see especially pages 58-68).

14. Donald R. Hands and Wayne L. Fehr, *Spiritual Wholeness for Clergy: A New Psychology of Intimacy with God, Self and Others*, foreword by Susan Howatch (Bethesda, MD: Alban Books, 1994), 54.

15. Ibid., 55.

16. Lovett H. Weems Jr., *Church Leadership: Vision, Team, Culture, and Integrity*, foreword by Rosabeth Moss Kanter (Nashville, TN: Abingdon Press, 1993), 122.

17. James E. Means, *Effective Pastors for a New Century: Helping Leaders Strategize for Success*, foreword by Bill Hull (Grand Rapids, MI: Baker Books, 1993), 217.

18. G. Lloyd Rediger, *Clergy Killers: Guidance for Pastors and Congregations Under Attack* (Louisville: Westminster John Knox Press, 1997), 133.

19. Ibid., 134-135.

20. George O. McCalep Jr., *Faithful over a Few Things: Seven Critical Church Growth Principles* (Lithonia, GA: Orman Press, 1996), 5.

21. W. E. Vine, *Vine's Expository Dictionary of New Testament Words,* Unabridged Edition (Peabody, MA: Hendrickson Publishers, N.A.), 502.

22. Carl Spain, *The Letters of Paul to Timothy and Titus (The Living Word Commentary)* (Abilene, TX: Abilene Christian University, 1984), 76.

www.ingramcontent.com/pod-product-compliance
Lightning Source LLC
Chambersburg PA
CBHW070933120626
46546CB00004B/1402